I0605470

TiNY TWEAKS, HAPPY LiFE

SIMPLE CHANGES to CREATE SPACE for WHAT MATTERS

ERIN PORT

ZONDERVAN®

Dedicated to Jesus—
my simplest and most
purposeful tweak

ZONDERVAN

Tiny Tweaks, Happy Life

Published by Zondervan, 3950 Sparks Drive SE, Suite 101, Grand Rapids, MI 49546, USA. Zondervan is a registered trademark of The Zondervan Corporation, L.L.C., a wholly owned subsidiary of HarperCollins Christian Publishing, Inc.

Requests for information should be addressed to customercare@harpercollins.com.

Zondervan titles may be purchased in bulk for educational, business, fundraising, or sales promotional use. For information, please email SpecialMarkets@Zondervan.com.

ISBN 978-0-3104-6655-0 (HC)
ISBN 978-0-3104-6657-4 (audiobook)
ISBN 978-0-3104-6656-7 (eBook)

Author is represented by Jenni Burke of Illuminate Literary Agency, www.illuminateliterary.com.

HarperCollins Publishers, Macken House, 39/40 Mayor Street Upper, Dublin 1, D01 C9W8, Ireland (https://www.harpercollins.com)

Art direction: Gabriella Wikidal

Printed in India

26 27 28 29 30 MAN 10 9 8 7 6 5 4 3 2 1

CONTENTS

INTRODUCTION

I ripped open the foil-covered gift with the eager hands of childhood, the anticipation of Christmas morning buzzing around me. I was in middle school, and my grandparents were visiting for the holidays. Inside, I found a stack of personalized notepads with my name printed boldly at the top, the blank pages ready to capture my thoughts. I squealed with delight, throwing my arms around my grandfather in gratitude.

I carefully stored those notepads with my collection of brightly colored Lisa Frank paper goods in my bedroom, determined to use every last page. My grandfather must have noticed how my sister, Ellen, and I would sneak into his home office years before to swipe similar notepads—freebies he kept for his customers. We'd spent a couple of summers living with our grandparents, and those simple pads of paper became a small yet meaningful connection between us. In fact, I would later start my own stationery company, with a few notepads inspired by the ones my grandfather had gifted me.

During those summers, we'd spend hours in their backyard, helping them tend their large garden. It's where my grandfather taught me to drive the rusty John Deere garden tractor, his hands gently over mine, guiding us as we mowed the horse pasture. My sister and I would sit together on their screened-in porch, coloring while our grandfather sipped his Diet Coke, one leg casually swung over the other, bouncing to his favorite big band music, his tube socks pulled halfway up to his knees. These moments, while simple, were the building blocks of a life filled with meaning and connection—and they deeply shaped who I would become.

Beyond the coveted notepads I received that Christmas, my grandparents rarely bought us gifts. Instead, they gave us the gifts of their time and presence. When my parents needed them to babysit, they wouldn't just stay home; they'd pack us up in their white Taurus, ready for adventure. When my grandfather's brother died in a military training accident, he stepped in as a surrogate father, paving the way for my dad to play a similar role in my cousins' lives (and planting the seeds in my own heart for adoption). When we were grown with families of our own, we'd spend every Thanksgiving in Florida with them, creating traditions of quality time together: collecting seashells, walking the beach, sharing stories, and laughing over french fries and mai tais. My grandparents gave us a legacy of moments that matter.

Years later, we found ourselves gathered around my grandfather's hospital bed, the antiseptic scent sharp in our noses, with wet tissues in hand as we dabbed at our tears. In his last moments on earth, the steady tone of the heart monitor beeped and whirled in the background, mingling with the familiar big band music we'd turned on—the same tunes we'd listened to as kids on the screened-in porch, now playing softly as we reminisced about all the happy, joyful moments of a life well lived. We took turns holding my grandfather's frail, wrinkled hand—the very one that had held mine so tenderly as he taught me to drive the tractor, the same hand I had grasped as we walked on the beach.

You know what we never talked about? How much money he had in the bank, whom he voted for in the last election, the size of his house, the car he drove, or the millions of other things that plague our minds and hearts daily. The hearse wasn't taking a bunch of his things or accomplishments to heaven with him. Most of those items would be packed into boxes, donated, or sold.

The end of life has a way of clarifying the truth of what really matters.

The end of life has a way of clarifying the truth of what really matters. As a young adult sitting through my aunt's memorial service, I wrestled with the realization that life was short. My grandfather's death years later reinforced the point. Both were catalysts that started my journey toward intentional living, ultimately leading me to embrace a life of purpose and simplicity. I wanted to figure out how to live meaningfully, how to find happiness and joy, and, eventually, how to show others how to do the same.

THE **PURSUIT** OF A **HAPPY LIFE**

I once overheard a lady at the DMV share that she was waiting for the day she could retire, get her pension, and live happily ever after. "I'm biding my time," she said. Is that really what life is all about? Grin and bear it in this season, hoping the next season will bring happiness? Wait for retirement to be happy, instead of looking for happiness now? Assume that job or that thing we're waiting for will bring us a happy life? Do we shuffle along, sad and without purpose, just biding our time?

The truth is that the lady in the DMV isn't alone. People aren't happy. American happiness has hit a fifty-year low, with only 14 percent of Americans reporting being very happy, the lowest level since this data was first tracked in 1972.[1] My heart ached when I read these numbers. I told my husband, "I want to help these unhappy people live well right where their feet are planted. Right here and now." Life is meant to be lived, loved, and enjoyed. Happiness isn't reserved for the occasional once-in-a-lifetime trip to Paris or some elusive future season. I had found the heartbeat of happiness and joy in my everyday life, and I wanted others to as well.

My mission became clearer everywhere I looked. Other parents at my kids' school and friends online asked me how I pulled it off with kids and a busy life. Their need to know how to live that meaningful life became the heartbeat of Simple Purposeful Living (SPL), the business I created in 2018. After years of working in education as a teacher and administrator, I made the decision to stay home to be a full-time mom and run SPL. In all my different jobs, I'd met women in every stage of life: single women, married women, moms, and women on the verge of retirement. No matter their life stage or experience, all had this one thing in common: They were overwhelmed by the complexities of life and bogged down by the day-to-day. Some were simply going through the motions, trying to keep their heads above water.

I've seen so many women wanting a simpler, happier life, but they were paralyzed by making a change. As we journey together through this book, I want you to keep one thing in mind: This isn't about striving for some unattainable ideal. It's about making small, intentional changes that lead to a more purposeful and joyful life that you love. We're going to dive into practical tips, personal stories, and simple tweaks that you can start applying today. By the end of this book, my hope is that you'll not only have a clearer sense of what brings you happiness but also the tools to create space for it in your everyday life.

CREATING A **LIFE** YOU **LOVE**

Who doesn't want small changes that create more space for happiness and fulfillment? I know it's tempting to dive in and try to make big changes all at once, but lasting change happens with steady, manageable steps. These tiny tweaks, done bit by bit, will add up over time to craft a life of joy without overwhelm.

This book is divided into four parts:

Part 1: The Pursuit of Happiness

We'll begin by helping you uncover what truly makes you happy. You'll explore what brings lasting joy and learn the power of tiny tweaks—small changes that align your life with your values. We'll also talk about flexing your fear muscle, because real change requires stepping out of your comfort zone.

Part 2: Minimize to Maximize

With the right mindset in place, we'll clear the clutter—both physical and digital. You'll learn how to minimize distractions and use time-trimming exercises to create space for happiness. The goal is to make room for what really matters, one small step at a time.

Part 3: Maximize the Moments

Now that you've created space, we'll focus on planning for what matters most. You'll build routines that help you show up with intention and maximize the moments that bring joy. These tweaks will reclaim your time so you can live more purposefully.

Part 4: Maintain the Momentum

In this final section, we'll address the sneaky obstacles that can derail your progress. You'll discover how tiny, consistent actions can keep you moving forward, even when life tries to stall your momentum. It doesn't have to be fancy to be effective. Small actions, done consistently, fuel progress and help you build a life you love, one simple step at a time.

Each chapter includes a tweak to try and a practical takeaway. I encourage you to work through them slowly. Small, steady steps lead to lasting change.

Ultimately, the goal of this book is to help you live a life you love right now. I want you to look back with pride, knowing you lived fully and purposefully. A life of connection, fulfillment, and happiness is available to us all. You have more control over this than you think. Now, let's get started.

Part 1
The Pursuit of Happiness

1

MIND YOUR MINDSET

We had waited more than two years for this moment—the day we would meet our youngest child, our son Quincy. We were huddled around a table with two other families in a stuffy boardroom on the tenth floor of an office building in Hefei, China. We watched as the other families were united with their children. A ten-year-old daughter would go home with her family to Tennessee, and a seven-year-old son would head off to Spain with his forever family. I cried tears of joy for them as we waited, looking up at the clock above the door every few minutes. We had already waited twenty-five months for our son, and every tick of the clock felt like another month as we held our breath.

When he finally came into the room, I reached out my hands. The nanny placed his fragile, listless body in my arms. He was so light, his eyes so hollow. As I held him, my heart felt like it would beat out of my chest. I whispered, "I love you," as I leaned in and he leaned away. Out of the corner of my eye, I happened to see another nanny laying a large pile of medications on the boardroom table. I thought to myself, *Someone's child is really sick*. Little did I know, those medications were for our child, and that moment marked the beginning of a long journey of finding help and healing for our son.

What we didn't know then was that our son had never eaten solid food. Although he'd already passed his second birthday, he weighed a whopping nineteen pounds, the average weight of a six-month-old in the United States. He could barely walk and spoke no words, not even in Mandarin.

When we arrived back in the United States, we tried to acclimate Quincy to life at "home"—a home where everyone and everything looked different—while simultaneously taking him to medical appointment after medical appointment. We'd spend an hour each meal trying to get him to eat solid foods, and he would often vomit it all back up. Because he was severely underweight, each day was literally a matter of life and death. I longed for him to gain a little weight, and I felt alone and so underqualified for this job of keeping him alive.

IN THE MIDST OF THE OVERWHELM

I was drowning, trying to care for Quincy's needs while also managing everything else life was throwing at me. I was treading water, gasping for air, and sinking fast. I eventually hit rock bottom after a difficult round of feeding and vomiting. After cleaning up Quincy and putting him in his crib for a nap, I closed his door and fell to my knees in the dark hallway. Tears trickled down my face. Exhausted and burned-out, I desperately wanted to escape from this season, but I was stuck, alone, with no way out.

Even if you haven't walked this exact road, I'm guessing you've had a moment when life felt like too much—whether it was the weight of a burden too heavy to bear, the exhaustion of juggling it all, or simply feeling stuck and unsure of the next step. In that moment for me, I felt paralyzed by overwhelm.

Have you ever seen those shows where crews of people come in, clear the clutter, and leave the house spotless, with happy homeowners waving as the credits roll? I wanted that—not just for my home but also for my schedule, my responsibilities, my problems, my fears. Where were Marie Kondo and that HGTV show when I needed them? How I longed to hear a knock on my door from a crew ready to help me overhaul my life.

No crew would come. But I didn't want this burned-out, drowning, overwhelmed existence. It wasn't serving me, and it wasn't serving my family. As tears streamed down my face in the dark hallway, a question popped into my head. It came from Emily P. Freeman's podcast that I listened to on our frequent trips to doctors' appointments: "What is the next right thing?"[1] Such a simple question, but instantly grounding when overwhelm had me in its grip.

I didn't want this burned-out, drowning, overwhelmed existence. It wasn't serving me, and it wasn't serving my family.

I went downstairs, brewed myself a cup of coffee, opened the sliding glass door, and stepped outside. The warmth of the sun on my skin felt like a small miracle, a little hug from heaven. I took a deep breath in and let the breath out slowly, and after several sips of coffee, I asked myself, *What is the next right thing?* That question became a tiny tweak to help me keep going.

WHAT IS A **TWEAK**?

Merriam-Webster defines a tweak as a small adjustment to something.[2] When we apply tiny tweaks to create a happier life, we're talking about making small adjustments to our mindsets, schedules, and households. We experiment, adjust, and improve, coming closer to what we want with a tweak here and there. Those small adjustments will then lead to big changes. What does that look like?

One of my kids' favorite recipes is my banana bread. But before it became beloved in our household, I went through a lot of batches to get it right. Does it need a little more salt? A little more spice? A little less flour? I spent time adjusting the cinnamon, nutmeg, sugar, and oil. I analyzed every ingredient and amount, and with each tiny tweak, the recipe got better and tastier. Then one day, as the kids and I cracked the eggs and a plume of flour erupted as they went into the mix, I decided to surprise everyone with one final tweak I knew they'd love: I added chocolate chips. (When in doubt, add chocolate. It's a good life motto in general.) It took fifteen versions, hours in the kitchen, (delicious) practice, and several small tweaks (we didn't love the version with extra nutmeg), but I ended up with a recipe that my family and I adore.

How does this apply to a happy life? Think of your life as a loaf of banana bread. You're not looking for a completely new recipe or a different kind of bread; you're focused on enhancing

YOU DON'T NEED TO OVERHAUL YOUR LIFE TO LOVE IT.

START WITH ONE SMALL TWEAK TO MOVE TOWARD A LIFE YOU LOVE.

the batter you already have. You want to make it richer, fuller, and more delightful—more uniquely yours. You might not have a clear vision of what makes you truly happy or what makes your life uniquely yours. You might be influenced by others' interests and experiences. But little by little, tweak by tweak, you can make small changes to shape a life that reflects what truly matters to you. Just as your banana bread might have nuts instead of chocolate chips, the beauty of tiny tweaks is that you can swap them and adjust your life into something that fits you perfectly. Each adjustment ideally adds flavor, texture, and joy, guiding you toward a more authentic and satisfying version of yourself.

Little by little, tweak by tweak, you can make small changes to shape a life that reflects what truly matters to you.

THE **POWER** OF A **TWEAK**

Out of the dark, low moments of my season caring for my new son, I discovered the true power of a tweak. I realized I had an unspoken expectation that I could handle everything the same way I did in a previous season, despite having more responsibilities and less capacity. I was trying to do too much and managing tasks that I didn't need to tackle alone.

One of the first tweaks I made was admitting I needed help—from my husband, family, and friends. When a friend asked, "Can I bring you dinner?" I said yes when I felt like I should say no. When a neighbor noticed our grass was overgrown, they mowed it and

I didn't interfere while I watched from the window, rocking Quincy and feeding him a bottle. When my husband, Scott, offered to do the laundry, I didn't view it as a slight to my abilities, as I might have before. I realized accepting help doesn't mean you've failed; it means you're not alone. Other tweaks I made at that time were adjusting my schedule to make room for simple things like writing in my gratitude journal, taking walks to enjoy the sun, establishing easy routines, and letting people in when I wanted to shut them out.

Maybe you've been in a similar place. Whether you're navigating a tough season or feeling overwhelmed by juggling the beautiful but demanding aspects of life, you're not alone. Life can be exhilarating and wonderful, but it can also stretch you to your limits and leave you feeling lost, overwhelmed, and lonely.

Even after recognizing the power of a tweak, the challenges didn't just go away. The day I fell to my knees, weeping, I understood that while my circumstances might not change, my approach to them could. A simple tweak allowed me to make tiny, manageable changes—one step at a time—that shifted my attitude in the short term and, over time, transformed how I experience life.

While my circumstances might not change, my approach to them could.

In making these small adjustments, I began to notice the deeper meaning in everyday moments. I realized that what had once been automatic now needed to become purposeful. A cup of coffee became more than just caffeine; it was a moment to pause and breathe amid the chaos. A walk wasn't merely exercise; it was an opportunity to enjoy the sun and reconnect with myself. These small, meaningful actions might have

THE IMPACT OF TINY TWEAKS

They can make things easier. Stephen Covey, in *The 7 Habits of Highly Effective People*, shared a story about a man working tirelessly to saw through a thick log. The blade grows dull, and a guy passing by suggests, "Why don't you sharpen your saw?" The man replies, "I don't have time; I'm too busy sawing."[3] It's a simple picture, but we've all been there—so busy doing the thing, we forget to tweak how we're doing it. But a small change can make everything run smoother. Maybe it's cleaning up the kitchen at night so your morning starts calmly. Or letting someone else handle a task you usually take on. Tiny shifts like these make life lighter and free up space for what really matters.

They can help you balance and adapt. Life's demands can feel overwhelming—like trying to balance all the dinner plates as you carry them to the table. It's tricky and stressful, and one wrong move could cause you to drop everything. But imagine you had a tray to carry them; suddenly the load is much more manageable. Small tweaks—like setting boundaries, creating a simple meal plan, or taking short breaks—are like that tray. They help you find balance and adapt to your season, making life easier without chasing perfection.

They can free you up to enjoy the journey. Embracing tweaks is like making tiny corrections while riding a bike—a slight tilt left, then right; pedaling faster, then slower. Small shifts can become second nature and help you navigate life's ups and downs. By focusing on intentional tweaks—like using a timer or carving out a few minutes for self-care—you simplify your days and enjoy the ride.

slipped by unnoticed in the hustle of caring for Quincy, managing my other kids, running a business, and keeping up with the house. But by simplifying, delegating, and cherishing these occasions, I found moments of joy again, *even in the midst of* a tough season.

Though the changes were tiny and nearly imperceptible at first, they guided me from wanting to escape a life I dreaded to embracing a life I loved. Circumstances didn't change—*I* did. With each small tweak, I transformed my life and fell in love with it along the way. Small tweaks are like those subtle adjustments that turn a basic banana bread recipe into a family favorite. They might seem minor, but they hold the power to make significant changes in your life.

When life gets hard, our instinct might be to long for someone else's seemingly perfect life and then want to overhaul everything so our life looks like theirs, but that's not necessary. You don't need a complete life transformation to find joy and fulfillment, and that would only leave you feeling more overwhelmed than you are right now. Small tweaks are all it takes to help you appreciate and love the life you're already living.

STAND UP, SISTER!

My grandmother screamed as if her life was in danger. I came around the corner at the lake to see that her blow-up plastic float had tipped over, leaving her floundering in the water. My mom was standing nearby, trying to help, but Grandma was panic-stricken because she didn't know how to swim and kept shouting, "I'm drowning!" My mom held out her hand and called, "Stand up!"

Grandma grabbed her hand and stood, the water lapping at her knees. She felt the stability of the lake bottom under her feet. She was okay.

Here I am telling you the same thing now: Stand up, sister! Sometimes we feel like we're drowning in the chaos of life, when all we need is a little nudge or someone to point out what we can't see for ourselves. Just like I needed Emily P. Freeman's words to help me find the next right thing, I want to help you create a life you love.

Sometimes we feel like we're drowning in the chaos of life, when all we need is a little nudge or someone to point out what we can't see for ourselves.

I found small tweaks that helped me wade through that tough season, moment by moment, day by day. Now I'm holding out my hand to you. Together, we're going to make tiny tweaks that will help you find solid footing again—sure and secure, no matter what you're walking through. You don't need to overhaul your whole life to love it. Sometimes a simple tweak is all it takes.

Grab my hand. We'll do it together. Are you ready? Stand up, sister—let's go!

5 TEENY-TINY TWEAKS TO SIMPLIFY LIFE TODAY

I want you to feel firsthand how a small change can make a big difference. Choose one tiny tweak to try—maybe one that solves a nagging issue like always losing your keys or your phone running out of battery. Start small and see how even a little shift can simplify your life and create momentum.

1. **Prep coffee the night before.** Set up your coffee maker in the evening so your morning starts smoothly and stress-free.
2. **Create a drop zone for essentials.** Designate a spot for keys and sunglasses—two of the biggest "hiders"—so you always know where to find them.
3. **Set up a charging station.** Plug in all your devices in one place before bed to ensure you and your electronics wake up fully charged and ready.
4. **Pre-pack bags.** Get work, school, or gym bags packed and ready the night before to avoid morning chaos.
5. **Run the dishwasher at night.** Load the dishwasher after dinner, run it overnight, and empty it in the morning to keep your counters and sink clutter-free all day.

2

WHAT MAKES YOU HAPPY?

What makes you happiest? Most filled with joy?" I asked my family these question on day six of our annual summer road trip. These questions were a little dangerous to ask, given that we'd been together on a tiny houseboat with a stinky marine toilet and cold-water showers for the past several days. We sat wrapped up in brightly striped beach towels in beach chairs, wet from our most recent swim to the sandbar, our toes tickling the sand, the waves of the Lake Michigan coast lapping in the background. We sipped cold cans of Coca-Cola and munched on turkey sandwiches filled with as much sand as turkey.

I asked them these questions then because that very moment was one of *my* happiest—outside with the warmth of the sun on my skin, surrounded by my family, the cares of the world far away. Curious how they answered?

"I'm happiest when I am at the lake." —Quincy (age 7)
"I'm happiest when I win." —Lucille (age 9)

"I'm happiest when I'm dancing." —Vera (age 13)
"I'm happiest when I'm plane spotting." —Solon (age 15)
"I'm happiest when I'm with you [Erin] and the kids, preferably outside." —Scott

I had to chuckle at their responses. Age has a way of clarifying what matters, doesn't it? The older I get, the more I find that what makes me happy is really quite simple. For me, in that moment, happiness was just the price of a tank of gas and a few groceries in exchange for sitting on the beach with my family. (Though I do like the satisfaction of winning a game of Qwirkle against Scott, so I have to agree with Lucille too.)

Have you ever thought about when you are happiest? The most joyful? Those moments when you pause for just a second and realize you have everything you need and feel content? Those moments when you want to freeze time? If I could bottle up moments like those and sell them, I'd be rich, because they are the true treasures of life.

If you're going to tweak your way to a life you love, it's important to know what truly fulfills you, what makes you happy.

If you're going to tweak your way to a life you love, it's important to know what truly fulfills you, what makes you happy. I know that sounds obvious, but maybe, like me, life has moved so fast that you haven't slowed down to think about it. Is happiness reserved for those rare, special moments when life slows down, or can we capture it in the ordinary, everyday bits of life?

I believe we can make space for more happiness, more joy, and more moments that matter—not just on special occasions but every single day. Sure, not every moment will be happy, but I'll bet we can find a little bit of joy in each day, even in the hardest seasons. And that's what takes a ho-hum life and makes it a vibrant one. When we know what truly makes us happy, we can pursue it with intention. Doesn't that sound like something worthwhile?

THE **CONNECTION** BETWEEN **JOY** AND **HAPPINESS**

For years I wrestled with the idea of pursuing happiness. Is it just a fleeting, never-ending chase? Is it a waste of time? Many of us believe happiness is tied to superficial and external things, like wealth, success, or material possessions, and when we chase them and don't find lasting happiness, it can make the pursuit seem pointless or shallow. But happiness, often reflected in external circumstances, gives us a glimpse into what truly matters and what brings us joy at a soul-deep level. It's like our heart's little alarm bell—*beep, beep, beep*—saying, "This! This is what matters." The day my family and I spent on the beach—as we played together, laughed, and enjoyed the sun and waves—the overwhelming sense of happiness I felt in that moment was more than a fleeting high. It was a moment of pure joy.

Happiness and joy are not the same thing, but they are intertwined. That's why when I refer to happiness in this book, I am referencing both together. Happiness

Happiness serves as a momentary signal for what brings your heart sustaining joy.

serves as a momentary signal for what brings your heart sustaining joy. It tells you what is deeply significant to you and reveals your values and purpose. Think of happiness as a clue to finding a priceless treasure. Why would you ignore something so valuable?

I want to be honest with you—happiness won't always be easy to find. I remember when I was nursing Quincy back to health. Those days seemed endless, and finding any kind of light required deliberate effort. But knowing what truly made me happy at the soul-deep level made the hard times easier. I learned to cling to the small moments—like a shared laugh or a friend bringing coffee so we could chat—to sustain me. Those hard seasons and dark moments made me appreciate true happiness and joy more. While what brings each of us happiness or joy will look different, there are common themes that can help us all—guideposts to help us notice and name what truly matters.

THE **GUIDEPOSTS** OF **HAPPINESS**

When I was in my twenties and teaching first grade, I would naturally praise my six-year-old students for their effort without much thought. But one day my principal left me a note after observing my class, pointing out how powerful it was to acknowledge their effort, not just the end result. That feedback brought a new level of awareness, and I started doing it on purpose, knowing it made a real impact on my students.

The same idea applies to happiness. We naturally gravitate toward what makes us happy, and we may be able to glean some benefits by default. But when we become *aware* of what truly

HAPPINESS

IS FOUND IN

EVERYDAY

MOMENTS.

brings us joy, we can be even more intentional about creating those moments more often. Remember that little alarm dinging and reminding you, "Hey, this really makes me happy. I should make time for this"? These happiness guideposts will help you notice your own "alarms" and become more intentional in pursuing what truly fulfills you.

HAPPINESS GUIDEPOST #1: COMMUNITY AND CONNECTION

I asked my Simple Purposeful Living (SPL) social media community what makes them happy. One common thread emerged when I looked at the responses: We are happiest when we're with others—when we have community and connection. Whether it's with our spouse, our kids, or our friends, our core relationships play a crucial role in our happiness.

Yet many of us are lonely. In another not-so-scientific Instagram poll, 69 percent (494 people) of our SPL community reported feeling lonely in the past week. This is a small sample, but it demonstrates that despite being more technologically connected than ever, we've never felt lonelier.[1] Studies suggest that around 20 to 30 percent of people report feeling lonely,[2] with women often experiencing higher rates,[3] as reflected in my poll. I've felt this pang of loneliness myself, especially when we moved to a new town in 2020 (which was not the best time for a move, as it turned out).

How do we combat loneliness and boost our happiness? The Harvard Study of Adult Development,[4] one of the longest and most comprehensive studies on human happiness, reveals that close, quality relationships are the strongest predictor of happiness and longevity—surpassing factors like wealth, fame, and professional success. This challenges the notion that more money or success will bring us true happiness. In a podcast interview, Shaquille O'Neal shared his experience of amassing $400 million in personal wealth, purchasing a 76,000-square-foot house, and achieving fame, only to realize that he had lost his family and close relationships along the way. He said, "You can have all the money in the world, but if you don't have anybody to share it with, it don't mean nothing."[5] To be truly happy, we need to surround ourselves with supportive people.

Marriage can be a great source of connection, but research has shown that women need community and connection beyond their spouse.[6] From talking to our SPL community, I know it can feel daunting to put yourself out there. Past pain and rejection can also make it difficult to want to try again. I've experienced painful friendship breakups that led me to believe I wasn't a good friend or worthy of friendship. Maybe you can relate. It's hard to reach out, to make small talk, to ask someone out for coffee, or to start a new relationship. It's also hard to feel lonely all the time. I had to ask myself, *Which hard would you rather choose?*

When we moved to our small town and I had to fill out emergency contact information for my kids' school, tears streamed down my face because I didn't have anyone to list. I realized I needed to put myself out there and build new friendships, not just for me but for my family. I knew from past experience that community brought comfort and joy, and I wanted that again. Even if you already have meaningful friendships and a full list of emergency contacts, remember that there's always room for more. Friends move, seasons change, and friendships evolve.

In Laura Tremaine's book *The Life Council*, she encouraged us to keep an "empty chair" at our friendship table, as you never know when you might meet a new friend.[7] You can never have too many, and not every friend needs to be your closest confidant. Friendship takes time to develop, but it starts with a small step. Take that step, and you'll be on your way to building meaningful connections that enrich your life.

Don't wait! Choose something. What will it be? If you want a truly rich life, you need to toss loneliness to the curb and find community. Putting yourself out there does require some effort on your part. Whatever you choose to do, initiate, be present, and relax. You can't find friends—and they can't find you—unless you're willing to be available and present.

HAPPINESS GUIDEPOST #2: PURPOSE AND MEANING

Do you have purpose and meaning in your life? Purpose can be a powerful indicator of happiness. It's not just about having a job or filling our days (like that DMV worker from the Introduction); it's about diving into activities that resonate deeply with us or make us truly feel alive. When I found something that ignited my passion, it was a game changer. I used to doubt the saying "Love what you do, and you'll never work a day in your life,"[8] until I started Simple Purposeful Living. Now, every morning I'm excited to dive into my work. It pulls me out of bed to craft another Instagram caption, and I'm often brainstorming ways to help others simplify as I fall asleep at night.

TINY TWEAKS TO HELP YOU FIND CONNECTION AND HAPPINESS

If this first guidepost for happiness reveals that you could use more community and connection, you may need some practical tweaks to get there. Whether you're lonely or not, try one of the following tweaks. After all, you could be the ray of sunshine in someone else's life today.

1. **Start small and local.** Open your eyes to people right in front of you. Your next friend may be a few yards away. Your neighbors. Your coworkers. People who attend the same gym classes or social groups. While it's great to keep in touch with those who are far away, you need people to do life with day-to-day, people you can name as emergency contacts. Maybe the small tweak you need is to keep your eyes open to a person you can say hello to right where your feet are planted.

2. **Don't judge a book by its cover.** Not all your friends will look like you or be in the same life stage. Don't limit your hellos to those you "think" would make a good friend. When someone approaches who seems different from people you're accustomed to, don't run the other way in fear. Say hello. Strike up a three-minute conversation. Not everyone you meet will become a close friend, and that's okay. But each conversation gives you an opportunity to practice asking thoughtful questions and showing genuine curiosity about someone new. With each hello, you'll grow a little braver and more confident for the next one.

3. **Attend events.** Participate in school, neighborhood, community, or work functions. My favorite place to pick up mom friends when I was a new stay-at-home mom was the local library. While it can feel overwhelming to go to an event where you don't know many people, it offers an organized opportunity, like preschool story time, to practice saying hello on neutral ground.

4. **Volunteer.** Take it a level deeper and get involved in school, church, or extracurricular committees or events as a volunteer. Working on a project with others relieves pressure to keep up conversation and gives you a focused goal while you get to know them.

5. **Join an interest group.** It might be a fitness class, a philanthropy group, a book club, a knitting club, or a Bible study. Like events, these groups and gatherings provide structure and take the pressure off you to coordinate hanging out. Plus, you'll automatically be meeting people who enjoy something you love.

Passion makes even the challenging days worthwhile, and let me tell you—you'll face many challenging days when you own a small business. I once had to trash hundreds of notepads that were glued instead of stickied together. I hated the waste, but my purpose to serve people well with a quality product sustained me and brought me joy.

Joy and purpose aren't limited to our work. You might find deep fulfillment in parenting. Watching your children grow, teaching them new things, and sharing special moments bring a profound sense of purpose. You can also find purpose in hobbies like gardening, painting, or volunteering. Remember that Instagram poll I conducted on happiness with my SPL community? Bethany feels happiest when she's deep into a project, whether it's restoring a piece of furniture, crafting a custom decor item, or transforming a space in her home. The process of taking something ordinary and making it beautiful fills her with a sense of purpose. Each project is a creative outlet that brings her joy, giving her direction and a deep sense of fulfillment as she sees her vision come to life. Another SPL community member, Ansleigh, finds happiness in the quiet escape of reading. Immersing herself in a good book provides her with a break from daily routines and a chance to connect with her passions.

Your purpose or passion could also be like that of my friend Carolyn, who volunteers her time to serve at-risk youth at a local after-school program. Carolyn finds immense joy in mentoring these young individuals, helping them navigate their challenges, and providing them with opportunities to succeed. Her work is a calling that gives her a profound sense of purpose. Knowing that she's making a positive impact in these young lives brings her deep satisfaction and happiness.

To discover what brings you joy and purpose, consider these reflective questions:

- What activities make you lose track of time because you're so engrossed in them?
- When do you feel most energized and fulfilled?
- Are there moments in your past when you felt truly proud and content? What were you doing?
- What aspects of your work, hobbies, or personal life make you feel like you're contributing to something larger than yourself?

As you reflect on these questions, remember that what your purpose looks like can evolve with different seasons. While I may no longer teach first graders, my passion for helping others continues to guide me. In this season you're in right now, how can you pour more into the pursuits that bring you joy and fulfillment?

HAPPINESS GUIDEPOST #3: CARING FOR YOURSELF

Two years after Vera, my second child, was born, I hit a wall. Exhausted and running on empty, I found myself sitting in the doctor's office, convinced something was seriously wrong. Vera had never slept through the night since her arrival, and I was utterly drained. The doctor ran every test under the sun, but they all came back normal. It was then that we had a heart-to-heart about my self-care.

While I knew the phrase "You can't pour from an empty cup," I was worried about what others might think if I took the time to refill mine. It didn't help that I was seeing posts online that debated the "empty cup" sentiment and suggested that new moms should be able to keep going. My doctor held my hand compassionately. A woman in her mid-sixties, she merged decades of medical knowledge and mature-woman wisdom as she reminded me, "Erin, a car can run on empty for only so long."

I recalled the night my mother-in-law and I were stranded on the side of the highway because her car had run out of gas. We should have stopped for gas as soon as the fuel light came on, but we ignored it and had to deal with the unfortunate consequences. My doctor acted as my warning light and gave me the permission I needed to care for myself so I could care for others, and I came up with a plan to fill my empty tank.

Even now I struggle with guilt that I should be doing more and that resting is somehow wrong. Resting can feel counter-cultural, almost like a guilty pleasure, but research shows that adequate rest is essential for our happiness and well-being.[9] Our weekends, which were once designed for rest, have become just two more days to hustle and catch up. It's no wonder we feel guilty when taking a break! But it's in those quiet moments that we find space to reflect, make tweaks, and care for ourselves. And that care seeps into all our other relationships, making us more patient, present, and joyful.

Maybe you're in that season where rest is harder to come by—where sleep is scarce because of little ones, or work is demanding every ounce of your energy. I've been there too. It's tough, and you might feel like there's no room to pause. But that's why it's even more crucial to grab those small pockets of rest when you can. Just because it's harder to come by doesn't mean it's any less important.

We can learn a thing or two from religions that promote the Sabbath as part of their regular rhythm. Rest is built into the week as a dedicated time to recharge because it isn't just an afterthought; it's a priority. Imagine if we treated rest as an essential part of our lives, like breathing or eating, instead of something to feel guilty about or squeeze in if we have the time.

Rest isn't selfish; it's essential.

I used to think rest was something I had to earn or needed permission for, but I've learned that rest is a gift. It's not just about feeling good; it makes me a better wife, mom, and friend. I have more patience, more presence, and more joy to give when I'm not running on empty. Rest isn't selfish; it's essential.

Here I am holding your hand and looking you in the eye: You and I are better wives, moms, and friends when we take the time to rest and care for ourselves. It's not about indulgences like pedicures or massages. True self-care is simpler. It's about making time for sleep, eating well, staying hydrated, exercising (even if at first it's just a walk around the block), and finding moments of calm amid the chaos. And let's not forget that even stillness and quiet can be self-care. Taking a few moments to sit in silence or to enjoy a calming cup of tea can be a powerful way to recharge. We don't always need to be *doing* something to care for ourselves. Sometimes just *being* is enough.

Sleep Can Make You Feel Your Best

After that day in the doctor's office, I realized that recognizing my need for sleep wasn't a luxury—it was a necessity. While some

TINY TWEAK
Simple Sleep Check

To figure out how much sleep you need, keep it simple:

- Jot down on a sticky note or your phone when you go to bed and when you wake up.
- Each day, mark a plus sign if you wake up feeling rested or a negative sign if you don't.
- Review your notes at the end of the week to see how much sleep you got and when you felt your best.
- Take the average of your sleep duration and adjust your bedtime accordingly.

Since most of us can't sleep in longer due to responsibilities, try setting an alarm on your phone to remind you when it's time for lights out. Remember, every week is different, so don't wait for the perfect week to start. Focus on making gradual adjustments to get closer to your ideal amount of rest so you can wake up feeling refreshed. Doesn't that sound amazing?

people might manage on less sleep, I've learned that I don't want to. I totally get it if you're rolling your eyes right now, especially if you're dealing with a child who doesn't sleep well, or caring for an elderly parent, or halfway through menopause. But for those of you who do have a choice, why settle for running on empty? Taking care of yourself is about more than just getting by—it's about truly thriving.

Research backs this up. The National Sleep Foundation recommends seven to nine hours of sleep per night for adults.[10] When we don't get enough rest, it's not just our mood that suffers—our overall well-being takes a hit. We're more prone to stress, irritability, lowered immunity, and fatigue.[11] Just like my kids, who turn into cranky bears when they don't get enough sleep, I've noticed I'm less patient and more on edge when I'm not well rested or properly nourished. I figured out that my body prefers eight hours of sleep, while my husband tends to need less, around seven hours. I used to feel guilty about needing more sleep than he did, until I realized we're all different, and that whatever the amount, rest makes us feel our best.

Since I'm up early on school days, my older kids now tuck me in at night, and they love this ritual as much as I do. Even my little ones look forward to the privilege of tucking in Mom someday. What I initially saw as a negative—needing more sleep—has turned into a special, cherished moment. This small, comforting ritual underscores the importance of taking care of myself while nurturing my well-being.

By finding the hours you need to operate at your best and creating a routine that supports it, you can ensure you're well rested and ready to embrace each day with happiness and energy.

Let the Sunshine In

Several years ago, inspired by my friend Crystal, I started to sit out on my back deck and let the sun's warmth hit my face. It seems too simple to make a difference, but sunlight also plays a crucial role in our mental health. Exposure to natural light helps regulate our circadian rhythm and boosts vitamin D and serotonin levels, which can improve our mood and alleviate symptoms of depression. Studies show that as little as ten minutes a day can be helpful.[12] Erin and Susan, two of our SPL community members, shared how getting consistent sunlight, walking, and spending time outdoors are essential for their happiness and balance. It's a powerful reminder that simple acts like soaking up natural light can profoundly impact our well-being.

Moving Your Body for Happiness

You might have mixed feelings about exercise, and I completely understand. I've been there myself. For years, exercise was about trying to shape my body into something I thought it should be, especially when I was struggling with an eating disorder. It felt like just another pressure to meet unrealistic standards. The world often makes exercise all about how we look, but I've discovered that exercise can be so much more than that. It can be a source of happiness.

During the pandemic, with gyms closed and everyone stuck at home, I started taking walks to manage stress and carve out some personal time. Those walks became my sanctuary, helping me feel happier, more content, and less stressed. I even slept better. If I skip a day of walking now, my digestion and mood definitely notice it. This tweak in perspective has been huge. Exercise is no longer about achieving a certain external body shape but about taking

TINY TWEAKS TO HELP YOU CARE FOR YOURSELF

Here are four tiny tweaks you can make:

1. **Set a consistent sleep schedule.** Determine the hours of sleep you need each night with the simple sleep check. There are also some great sleep apps, monitors, and wearable tech that can help.
2. **Get some sunlight.** Spend at least five to ten minutes outdoors each day, especially in the morning, to boost your mood and regulate your sleep–wake cycle.
3. **Stay hydrated.** Drink plenty of water throughout the day. I like putting slices of lime and lemon in mine to add flavor, and I tend to drink more water when it's in a bottle. Apparently, so does Quincy, who's always stealing a drink out of my water bottle.
4. **Move your body.** Find an activity you enjoy, whether it's walking, dancing, or yoga, and make time for it regularly. Even short bursts of physical activity (five to ten minutes) can boost your energy and mood. If I am feeling tired in the afternoon, a quick walk around the block perks me up.

care of myself and improving my internal well-being. It's a vital part of my self-care routine, boosting my mood and overall happiness, and it's been incredibly freeing to embrace movement for what it truly offers me internally.

Research shows that just ten to thirty minutes of moderate physical activity each day—like dancing to your favorite songs, doing a quick stretching routine, or fitting in some body-weight exercises like squats, push-ups, and lunges—can significantly boost your mood and overall health. These activities are easy and effective and can be done anywhere.[13] The goal is not to add stress by giving you another thing to do, but to find a type of movement that enhances your well-being and fits into your life in a supportive way. It might take a little experimentation, but prioritizing this simple form of self-care is a key part of living a well-rounded life.

Taking care of your body isn't just about avoiding illness—it's about ensuring you have the vitality to enjoy and engage with life fully. Maybe, like me, you can recall a time when your body was telling you, "You're running on empty." Just like we ensure our cars receive a little maintenance to get us where we need to go, we can make tiny tweaks to take care of ourselves and notice how they enhance our overall well-being and ultimately make us happier and healthy.

HAPPINESS GUIDEPOST #4: CONNECT WITH **NATURE**

As I sat with my family on the Michigan shoreline, soaking in the sun and sharing what made us happy, it was clear that being outdoors played a significant role in our well-being. Those moments of tranquility and connection with nature were not just fleeting feelings—they aligned with what we know works. Many members of my wonderful SPL community echoed similar sentiments. Brooke finds joy in camping in nature and vacation time with family, while Beth feels happiest when near water. Why is nature so valuable to our happiness?

When we get outside and connect with nature, we're tapping into a fundamental source of joy and balance.[14] It's not just about enjoying a pretty view; it's about giving ourselves the opportunity to reset and recharge. So as we continue to explore what brings us happiness, remember the simple yet powerful impact of the great outdoors. Whether you're going for a walk in the park or spending time in your garden, make space for these experiences. They're more than just refreshing. They help you to be present in the moment. Take in the beauty around you; it's essential for a well-lived life.

HAPPINESS CAN BE FOUND IN THE EVERYDAY

Happiness isn't reserved for special occasions. This is good news, since most of life takes place between those. Some of our happiest moments will rise to the top because of intensity or novelty, but I believe we can find happiness in our everyday lives if we're mindful of it. By focusing on the essential elements of a well-lived life, we can discover joy not only during vacations or special events but also in small, simple moments.

When I find myself tempted by the allure of material gains,

TINY TWEAKS TO TAKE IN NATURE

1. **Take a quick walk.** Stroll around your neighborhood or local park.
2. **Sit outside.** Enjoy time on your porch or patio. Take a few deep breaths and notice your surroundings. What do you see? Hear? Smell? Feel?
3. **Open the windows.** Let in fresh air and listen to the sounds of nature.
4. **Garden.** Spend a few minutes tending to your plants or garden.
5. **Watch the sunrise or sunset.** Take a moment to appreciate the beauty of dawn or dusk.
6. **Bird-watch.** Observe local birds and note their activities.
7. **Sit on a bench.** Find a local bench and take a short break in a natural setting.
8. **Picnic.** Have a mini picnic with a coffee, snack, or meal outside.
9. **Read outdoors.** Read a book or article outside for a few minutes.
10. **Stargaze.** Take a moment to look up at the stars or clouds.
11. **Build a snowman.** Embrace your inner child and build a snowman. It's a fun activity for all ages and a great way to enjoy the snow. Or skip the snowman and have a snowball fight.
12. **Sled.** Head to a nearby hill with a sled or toboggan for some thrilling downhill fun. It's a simple and exciting way to enjoy the winter weather.

success, wealth, or the next "big thing," I tell myself to step away from the comparison and distraction. I remind myself what truly brings happiness and joy. I spend time outdoors, connect with others, and engage in activities that align with my passions and purpose. Material possessions can provide temporary satisfaction, but the meaningful experiences and relationships we cherish offer lasting joy. True contentment comes from appreciating these deeper aspects of life, not from chasing after external markers of success.

Our mood is magnetic.

Here's another thing I've learned: Our mood is magnetic. When we focus on happiness and make it a priority, it transforms not only us but also those around us. Emotions like joy and enthusiasm are contagious, spreading through our words, our actions, and even our energy. You know that person who radiates genuine joy (not forced positivity but real joy)? You want to be around them because their happiness is uplifting. When you choose to prioritize happiness, you're not just helping yourself; you're inspiring others too.

HAPPINESS SQUARE

Start a daily joy practice by spending a few minutes each day doing something that brings you happiness. Not sure where to start? Identify a few ideas in each of these areas.

Connect with Others
Ideas and activities I enjoy that foster meaningful relationships and connections:

Live Your Purpose
Activities that align with my passions (work, volunteering, hobbies):

Rest and Recharge
Ways I enjoy relaxing to rejuvenate my mind and body:

Nature and Joy
Activities that help me connect and find joy outdoors:

3

WHAT MATTERS MOST TO YOU?

I'd never ridden a bullet train but had always wanted to, so I was excited to ride at crazy speeds across the countryside in China from Beijing to Hefei on our way to adopt our younger son. As we took our seats, I noticed a digital sign above the sliding door of the train car that displayed our speed. Once we were moving, I looked up at one point and did a double take. We were going 384 kilometers per hour, roughly 238 miles per hour!

The ride was relatively smooth as we glided along the tracks. Outside the window, the landscape whizzed past. We were moving so fast that anytime one of us would point out something interesting, by the time the rest of us looked, we had missed it. I tried to snap photos, but each shot was blurry. When the train finally slowed down, I could truly take in the scenery and shoot clear pictures through the window. We oohed and aahed at tall building after tall building, the large city coming into focus.

Life, like that bullet train, moves fast, and we can miss so much if we let it go by. And it turns out that the older you get, the faster it moves. When my friend Larry first mentioned that to me, I was still in my early twenties. The world before me was full of possibilities, a blank book ready to be filled with experiences. However, as I have aged, I've come to understand this sentiment more and more. Our elder son is on the cusp of moving out and heading to his next adventure. (I'm going to need a minute. Let me find a tissue.) The baby boy I once held in my arms is now a muscular high school athlete who looks more like a man—reminding me daily just how fast life moves. Moments slip by, hardly seen or felt before disappearing in our rearview mirror. We must learn how to intentionally slow down our train to be sure we're on the right track and focus on what matters the most to us in the blur of life.

We must learn how to intentionally slow down . . . and focus on what matters the most to us.

SAVOR THE MOMENTS

In the previous chapter, we dug into how those fleeting moments of happiness—whether spent with loved ones, immersed in nature, or engaged in self-care—are more than just passing events. They serve as signals, pointing to the deeper values and joys in our lives. These moments reflect what truly matters to us, but simply recognizing them isn't enough. That's just the first step. To live lives that are not only full but deeply fulfilling, we need to weave

To live lives that are not only full but deeply fulfilling, we need to weave these joyful experiences into the fabric of our everyday existence.

these joyful experiences into the fabric of our everyday existence. How do we do that?

One of the most effective tools to find happiness in our everyday experience is practicing gratitude. It's not just about saying thank you but really embracing and recognizing the lessons and blessings in every season of our lives. While incorporating gratitude might seem like a small tweak, it has a lot of power. Just as slowing down on a speeding train allowed me to truly appreciate the scenery, incorporating gratitude into my daily routine helped me slow down and savor those everyday moments of meaning.

In those challenging days of nursing Quincy back to health, I found that what I focused on mattered. When I focused on my overwhelming situation, all the things I could not control, I broke down, feeling defeated. When I focused on the next right thing, my beautiful son, and a simple cup of coffee, I could breathe a little easier—even though my circumstances hadn't changed at all. As Charles R. Swindoll wisely said, "You can't always change your circumstances, but you can change your attitude."[1] By acknowledging the good in our lives, even the good that comes out of the hard or unexpected—the lessons, the growth, the resilience—we shift our focus from what's missing to what's present, creating a ripple effect of joy. While not every day might be a good day, I have learned there's good to be found in every day. It's just a matter of what we are looking for—and gratitude gives us the eyes to see.

STEPS TO **TWEAK** FOR **GRATITUDE**

Step 1: Uncover Joy in the Everyday

Years ago, after suffering a miscarriage and facing the heartbreak of not getting pregnant again, I found myself trapped in a painful thirty-day cycle of hope and disappointment. It was during this season that I came across *One Thousand Gifts* by Ann Voskamp.[2] Her words about the transformative power of gratitude struck a chord with me. Voskamp shared how noticing and appreciating the beauty in everyday life, even amid challenges, could bring deep joy. Inspired by her journey, I began my own practice of finding one thousand gifts, writing down a few things I was grateful for each day.

Over the next several months, while our circumstances remained unchanged, my perspective began to shift. I started to notice the small joys that had always been there: the morning snuggles with my kids, a warm cup of coffee by an open window, an encouraging phone call from my mom. This practice became so impactful that I eventually designed a gratitude journal for our shop to share this life-changing habit with others.

Life, as it often does, got busy, and when Quincy came home, the demands of caring for him caused me to let the practice slip. But as I navigated the challenges of nursing Quincy back to health, I remembered how much this practice had helped me before. So I picked it up again, this time with renewed intention. I was able to see moments of joy even in the midst of those difficult days. One day I wrote:

> I am thankful for the moment today when he finally leaned in for a hug. Quincy let out the cutest belly laugh. Everyone around the table for dinner. A warm cup of coffee I didn't need to reheat

today. A shower and fresh clothes. Getting outside and playing in bubbles while Quincy wore Lucille's pink bike helmet.

You might be tempted to skim through this book, picking out tips to make life easier. While those tips are here, they're about more than just simplifying life. They're about creating space with intention and discovering what to fill that space with—the things that make your life feel rich and fulfilled. Before we can make that space, we need to uncover what really matters to us in our daily lives.

Think of it like decluttering a closet. You wouldn't start without knowing which items you truly love and want to keep. Maybe you keep your favorite cozy sweatshirt that always feels just right but let go of that scratchy sweater everyone raved about on social media—even though it never quite suited you. The same goes for life. It's not just about clearing out what doesn't belong but about thoughtfully deciding what does. What brings you joy might not be what everyone else values, and that's perfectly okay.

In the previous chapter, we began this process of discovery, providing a resource to get you thinking about the guideposts of happiness: connecting with others, caring for yourself, aligning with your purpose, and spending time in nature. Now we're going to dig deeper into what this looks like in your day-to-day life. By practicing gratitude, we can slow down, notice what truly enriches our lives, and make intentional tweaks to create space for those things.

Let's start by setting up a simple, impactful practice.

Step 2: Find Connections to Confirm Your Priorities

As you dive into your gratitude practice, you'll start to see how writing down what you're thankful for reveals tiny, meaningful

TINY TWEAKS TO PRACTICE GRATITUDE

1. **Set up your practice.** This week, carve out a few moments to start. Grab a notebook, your phone's Notes app, or even just some paper—don't overthink it. Set a daily alarm labeled "gratitude journal" and keep the journal in a place where you'll see it regularly. These small reminders will help you stay consistent.
2. **Reflect daily.** Each day, take a few minutes to write down three to five things you're grateful for. It could be a moment, an interaction, or something simple that brought you joy. Do this for at least a week and notice how it begins to shift your perspective.

This practice isn't just about listing what you're grateful for; it's about learning to recognize and prioritize what truly brings you joy so you can intentionally create more space for those things in your daily life.

ways your priorities show up in your daily life. The more I wrote, the more I noticed how even more of what mattered to me manifested in my daily life. My journal captured moments of purpose and joy that might otherwise have been overshadowed by the failure to get pregnant. I found mindfulness begets mindfulness; the more intentionally I looked for what mattered to me, the more

The more intentionally I looked for what mattered to me, the more I found it.

I found it. This time of self-reflection was a tweak I didn't know I needed in more than one challenging season. My priorities and what mattered to me gradually became crystal clear.

I flipped through the numbered list, looking for connections and themes, in hope of recognizing what truly mattered to me. In time, my priorities became obvious.

Here's an example of my priorities, manifested in daily and weekly activities recorded in my journal:

Family: family dinners, early-morning bedhead snuggles, playing games, bike rides, hikes outside, playing with bubbles and sidewalk chalk

Marriage: walks with Scott, date nights, evening chats

Health: early-morning coffee time, a good night of sleep, daily walks, windows open, tending my garden, sitting in the sunshine

Friendship: lunches, story time at the library, MOPS (Mothers of Preschoolers), chats with my sister, Ellen

Now you give it a try. Review your gratitude journal and see what connections you can find, what priorities are consistently showing up—or are missing. Grab a few highlighters and color-code them by priority—maybe pink for connection, yellow for self-care, and green for nature. Look at the pages and see if one color stands out more. Are there themes? Anything surprise you that was written down? What about things you *didn't* write down?

What I hope you discover is that much of what you're doing already aligns with your priorities, and you can approach these activities with even more intention. When you understand what matters and why, you're naturally inclined to make time for it.

As you continue this practice in the future, you might find that something that was once represented, like time with friends, has been missing for a few weeks. If you're finding that some areas need more attention, this is your chance to tweak your life and be sure your values are reflected, even in tiny ways. By slowing down and assessing your priorities, you can adjust your course and make more time for what matters.

Step 3: Determine What's Not Needed

When my eldest was little, I used to go all out for birthdays with elaborate parties because I thought that's what I "should" do. Over time, I've learned that sometimes the best tweak is letting go of what we feel we should do just because it's expected or because everyone else is doing it. We often hold on to things that no longer serve us. In Greg McKeown's book *Essentialism*, he teaches us that to live a truly fulfilling life, we need to focus on what really matters and eliminate what doesn't.[3] This principle became clear to me as I reflected on my gratitude journal. It's not just about recognizing the moments that bring joy; it's also about noticing what's missing. Those birthday party themes weren't listed.

During my season of infertility, I found that stepping away from MOPS was a necessary tweak. The constant pregnancy announcements were too painful for me at that time. While it had been a huge blessing to meet other stay-at-home moms when I first stayed home, it no longer served me well in this new season. Recognizing

TINY TWEAKS FOR ADDRESSING WHAT'S MISSING

As you think about what's missing and what matters, consider how you could start to tweak in the easiest possible ways. Here are some ideas to get you thinking:

- If you're missing quality time with one kid, set up a "date" and add it to one of your regular errands. Grab a hot chocolate together on the way to the grocery store or let them pick a song to blast in the car while you drive to an appointment.
- If you're missing alone time, try waking up fifteen minutes earlier for a quiet moment with your coffee, taking a short walk after dinner, or keeping a book in your bag to sneak in a few pages while waiting in the school pickup line.
- If you're missing quality time with your husband, plan something simple but intentional: an after-bedtime dessert date at the kitchen table, a walk around the neighborhood, or even tackling a small home project together with music and conversation. It doesn't have to be elaborate to be meaningful.
- If you're missing time with friends, send a quick text and set up something easy: a coffee catch-up, a walk, or even a phone call while folding laundry. Sometimes we just need to make the first move.
- If you're missing creative time, set out your supplies in plain sight so it's easier to start—even if it's just for ten minutes.

The beauty of a tweak is that it's *easy*. By taking time to write in your gratitude journal, you'll not only start to see what matters, but you'll also be able to intentionally focus on making small adjustments to align your life more closely with what matters to you.

when something that once brought value no longer fits is an important part of prioritizing what truly matters.

Take a look at your gratitude journal and your calendar. What's on your calendar that's not showing up in your gratitude journal? Reflect on what you're doing because you think you "should" rather than because it genuinely aligns with your current priorities. Understand that even good things, like MOPS or fancy birthday parties, may not fit every season of your life. That's okay. What matters most is making room for what truly enriches your life right now.

Recognizing when something that once brought value no longer fits is an important part of prioritizing what truly matters.

By recognizing what's not serving you, you can make space for what does. This tweak will help you focus on what genuinely brings you joy and fulfillment, allowing you to live a more intentional and satisfying life.

Step 4: Do More of What Matters

Now that we've cleared away what doesn't matter, let's turn our attention to focusing on what truly does. This is where we intentionally introduce new activities if needed and make thoughtful adjustments to the activities we already do.

For years, I thought regular date nights with my husband were out of reach due to our busy lives and the expense of hiring a babysitter. We'd manage a night out every other month at best. But spending time together was important to us and was reflected in my gratitude journal, so I decided to make a tweak. I realized dates don't need to include food. This was a profound aha moment for me. We began taking weekly walks. When the kids were younger, we'd strap them into the stroller or let them bike ahead, and as they got older, we walked around the neighborhood while our eldest child kept an eye on the younger ones. This simple tweak to our time together meant we were dating way more.

Another tweak we made was to ensure we read to our youngest two kids as we had with the older ones, even though we were so much busier. To do this, we set an alarm for 7:45 p.m. to signal bedtime. Initially, we struggled to fit reading into our routine amid the busyness, but knowing it was important, from reviewing my gratitude journal, helped us adjust. While we're not perfect, we're reading more often, thanks to this small, intentional tweak.

Look at your own gratitude journal. Are there areas of your life that you'd love to focus on more? What's something important to you that's currently missing? Think about how you can make intentional adjustments. In part 2 we will create even more time for what matters, but for now simply changing your mindset—like realizing that date nights don't need to involve food—will make a huge difference. My husband and I now have two walking dates each week, and we barely miss them because cost and energy aren't an issue.

Step 5: Don't Tweak What's Not Broken

The other day, my cousin Madelynne shared about her fitness program. I'm a happy daily walker, but the urge to make a tweak hit me at that moment. I wondered, *What if her way is better? What if I can get more fit?* The grass suddenly looked greener on the other side. But I held to a principle I've learned the hard way: Don't tweak what's not broken.

IDENTIFY WHAT MATTERS MOST TO YOU SO YOU CAN TWEAK YOUR WAY TO A LIFE WITH INTENTION.

Avoid the urge to overtweak or tweak something that doesn't need it. You're going to be bombarded by ideas, tips, and tricks online. You'll get more Pinterest inspiration and TikTok tutorials than you could possibly ever use, and you'll have to discern what you actually need. If you click Like on an Instagram post about simplification, the algorithm will dish you up another hundred. Resist trying them all or you'll find yourself with a more complicated life than ever. Next thing you know, you'll end up right back where you started, overwhelmed and drowning. Remember that the best tweaks simplify your life and help you focus on what matters.

The best tweaks simplify your life and help you focus on what matters.

Take in the information and test it out. With trial and error, you'll be like Goldilocks in her search for the just-right bed, tweaking your way to the just-right life.

A LIFE OF **KNOWING WHAT MATTERS** MOST

Since life moves so fast, gratitude not only helps us slow it down but also helps us create a lifelong practice of making moments matter—and those moments lead to more moments, and ultimately to a lifetime of moments. Annie Dillard said, "How we spend our days is, of course, how we spend our lives. What we do with this hour, and that one, is what we are doing."[4] Our present moment of gratitude is creating in us a lifetime of gratitude.

Slow down the train, start writing down what you are grateful for, take in the scenery, and check that you are on the right track. Make sure how you spend your days is how you want to spend your life. Let go of what doesn't work and what doesn't matter, and make tiny tweaks to make what matters happen in the easiest way possible. Over time, you'll find that a tweaked life is indeed a happier life because it aligns with what matters most to you.

Let go of what doesn't work and what doesn't matter, and make tiny tweaks to make what matters happen in the easiest way possible.

But that doesn't mean it's easy. Changes, even tiny ones, can be scary. So let's care for ourselves by doing what matters, what brings us joy, and next we will learn how to flex our fear muscle . . . one tweak at a time.

GRATITUDE PRACTICE

This week, write in a gratitude journal or notebook to identify what matters to you. Then walk through the five steps in this chapter to hone your gratitude practice.

Step 1: Uncover Joy in the Everyday. Write down three to five things you're grateful for. They could be a moment, an interaction, or something simple that brought you joy.

Step 2: Confirm Your Priorities. Look for connections and themes to confirm your priorities and recognize what truly matters to you.

Step 3: Determine What's Not Needed. Take a look at your gratitude journal and your calendar. What's on your calendar that's not showing up in your gratitude journal? What are you doing because you think you "should" rather than because it genuinely aligns with your current priorities?

Step 4: Do More of What Matters. What areas of your life would you love to focus on more? What's something important to you that's currently missing? Think about how you can make intentional adjustments.

Step 5: Don't Tweak What's Not Broken. Is there anything you're trying to tweak that doesn't need it?

4

FLEX YOUR FEAR MUSCLE

My palms were sweaty inside my little neon pink, yellow, and green gloves as I stood in line for the ski lift with my dad. With bib numbers pinned to our brightly colored, early-nineties ski coats, we slid up to the mark and waited for the lift operators to pull the T-bar beneath our bottoms to carry us and our skis to the top of the mountain. Our skis followed the grooves in the snow as we went up and up. My little eight-year-old heart started beating out of my chest as I looked to my left and saw the ski course all marked out. Racers sped as fast as they could between the poles. It would be my turn soon.

We had moved to Switzerland the summer before, and every Friday for gym class I took ski lessons in the Swiss Alps. (I know. Who gets to say that?) I learned all the basic skills, and being young and reasonably unafraid, I picked up these skills quickly.

This particular weekend, however, was different. We were at our favorite little local ski place, La Lécherette, for a family ski day and competition hosted by our school. As my dad and I waited for our turn, a churning stomach joined my accelerated heart rate and sweaty palms. Tears welled, and my cheeks grew pale as we inched closer to the starting line. I'd skied this course a hundred times, but today I'd be timed in the school race. *What if I fall and everyone sees me? What if I fail and get last place? What if I hit one of the poles?*

They called our names, and I froze. My dad tried to usher me along, now realizing how pale I was. He told the gate attendant we needed a moment, so we slid to the right to let others go by. He bent low, looked into my eyes, and listed everything a parent says: "You've done this a million times before." "It's no big deal." "It will be less than a minute." "We have to ski down."

But I didn't end up racing that day.

Fear got the better of me. I hadn't yet built up my fear muscle. While fear is built into us to keep us safe so we don't get eaten by a bear or fall off a cliff, sometimes we fear things that mean us no harm. The fear of the unknown, the fear of what others might think, the fear of judgment, failure, and rejection. And just like me on that hill, we let fear keep us comfortable in the known rather than uncomfortable in the scary unknown, even if what's on the other side is better.

We let fear keep us comfortable in the known . . . even if what's on the other side is better.

All those fears don't just disappear when we move into adulthood. Fast-forward thirty years to when we went to adopt our son. I knew there was no turning back. I was terrified, but I walked with confidence into the office building where they placed my baby boy in my arms. How did I go from being too afraid to ski down the mountain to stepping into fear to go get my son? We don't suddenly get brave. I had to strengthen my fear muscle over time, gradually making courageous decisions to step into the fear instead of staying stuck in my comfort zone.

STRENGTHEN YOUR FEAR MUSCLE BY **STARTING SMALL**

We must learn to flex our fear muscle to achieve our goals and grow into stronger, more confident women who don't miss out on full and fulfilling lives. It starts with strengthening that fear muscle. We're not naturally wired to face down fear. We were born with a fight-or-flight instinct. When we sense fear, we instinctively want to run the other way. When asked to change, we naturally shake our heads, wanting to stay in our comfort zones, but that leads to missing out on new experiences and a better life.

To overcome the instinct to turn back, to resist, we can start small, flexing our fear muscle in tiny ways. It's like when you begin lifting weights at the gym. You don't start with twenty-pound dumbbells. Start with the five-pound weight. Get some reps in. Eventually, you can pick up the ten-pounder and then the fifteen-pound dumbbell. You get a little stronger over time, a little more sure of yourself.

Are you afraid to make new friends? You don't have to invite people over for a three-course meal. Start small. Just say hello or sit next to someone at your child's activity and compliment their kid. Have you always wanted to learn how to bake bread but you're scared by the commitment of a sourdough starter? You

It takes courage to make changes.

don't need to start with sourdough. Look up an easy bread recipe online and try it. Want to run a 5K but feel daunted by the physical effort? Start with running for a few minutes. These little actions and subsequent successes prove to your brain that you can face your fear and survive. They add up to more evidence and build the confidence you can rely on when you face a bigger fear and feel like running away scared.

To arrive at the happy life we long for, we might think we need to chuck this one and get a whole new life, but that's not necessary. Instead, we can start making tiny tweaks, and with one small, brave action after another, we find that change isn't so scary. It takes courage to make changes.

A little nudge here and a little nudge there will help you flex your fear muscle with the least resistance. Over time, you'll confidently step outside your comfort zone and into a life you love. With each tweak, you may start to feel that old familiar fear knock on the door. You may want to quit, to go back to the way things were. But you don't grow in your comfort zone, so when you feel fear creeping up, let it encourage you to keep tweaking. Feel proud that you're growing, stepping out of your comfort zone, and bravely forging a path forward.

You know what I learned from that fateful day on the ski slope? The sting of regret is far greater than the fear of the moment. As a grown woman, whenever I visit my dad's office, I now hold the gold metal frame of a picture of my dad and me at the top of the ski slope. Decades older than the girl who panicked, I remember how I felt when I gave in to my fears. I wish I'd skied down that hill, even if I had come in last. I wish I'd known then what I know today about fear. As I place that photo back on the shelf, I smile because it reminds me not to let my feelings prevent me from taking action, even if the outcome isn't perfect.

LET YOUR **ACTIONS** FORM YOUR **FEELINGS**

Do you know the most common day to start something new? Tomorrow! Do you know why? We hope we will feel like it tomorrow. Marie Forleo, in her book *Everything Is Figureoutable*, said, "Fear is not the enemy. Waiting to stop feeling afraid is."[1] We may never feel like trying something new, but that shouldn't stop us from acting. Just like when you walk inside on a sunny day and it takes a few minutes for your eyes to adjust, when you flex your fear muscle, it takes a few moments for your emotions to catch up with your actions.

We've all been in new seasons where we miss the old ones. We add a child to our family, and we reminisce about when it was easier and we felt more sure of ourselves. We switch jobs and crave the old one, even though we hated it, just because everything feels new and different now. We've taken some kind of action, and we need to give ourselves a minute to adjust to the new normal. Every time my family moved when I was growing up—and we moved every two years—my dad used to say, "It's not good or bad, just different." As we settled into our new normal, we'd long for the old house, the old school, the old friends. But with time, we'd find our footing, and different would become the new normal.

It's the same for you. Next time you're about to try a tweak and you feel scared, worried that it'll fail, remember: It's not good or bad, just different. Acknowledge your feelings, but don't let them keep you stuck. Then take action—and let the feelings follow.

THE **FIRST TIME** IS THE HARDEST

My elder son asked me to jump off the high dive with him at the local pool a few years ago. I was in my thirties and had never jumped off a high dive before. I had always been too scared. But when he looked at me with those sweet hazel eyes, I decided I could flex my fear muscle for him.

My legs trembled as I climbed the ladder and waited my turn. I looked over the edge way down at the pool below, took a deep breath, and jumped. I came to the surface gulping in air, exhilarated. It was amazing! I'd spent more than thirty years fearing the high dive, and it turns out that the fear and anticipation were much worse than reality. *Why had I waited so long?* After my son had his turn, I immediately asked if he wanted to go again. The second time wasn't nearly as scary.

The first time you try something, it's the hardest and scariest because it's unknown. Your first time behind the wheel of a car, your first date, your first time flying, your first time giving birth. All are hard and scary, but they get easier. The first time you make a recipe, you might need to read over it several times as you move slowly, following the steps carefully, afraid you'll mess it up. But the steps become easier each time you take them, until you have them figured out and feel confident, even fearless.

It's the same with flexing your fear muscle in a new area: It will get easier each time. As kids, we were beginners and had so much to learn. As adults, we don't always allow ourselves to be beginners again. We don't give ourselves the grace to try because we think we should have it all figured out. News flash: We're all still just trying to figure it out. We want to be perfect right out of the gate, but making progress takes time and practice. Don't let the fear of not being perfect rob you of the process. Remember, the first time is always the hardest, but you'll learn from the experience. When you start to anticipate what negative things might happen, recall how anticipation was worse than reality in the past. That jump off the high dive wasn't so bad. I survived. Take the plunge. And grab a friend, because flexing your fear muscle is so much easier when you have someone by your side.

Making progress takes time and practice. Don't let the fear of not being perfect rob you of the process.

WHO'S YOUR **PERSON** WITH THE **POM-POMS**?

I'll never forget the night I rolled over and told Scott I wanted to start Simple Purposeful Living. I'd blogged for years but finally knew what I wanted to focus on. We were in bed, and he was nearly asleep as I shared my big news. He kissed me on the cheek and told me he believed in me and that I should go for it. Then he rolled over and promptly started snoring. He doesn't remember that moment, but I do. Even half asleep, he shook figurative pom-poms and cheered me on when I needed it the most—and continued to the next morning and for all these years. He gave me the courage to flex my fear muscle when I wasn't sure I had what it took.

Facing your fears isn't easy, but the more support you have, the more likely you'll be to succeed.

When we face new opportunities and choose to step outside our comfort zone, having a supportive network of people to cheer us on isn't just a nicety but a necessity. Facing your fears isn't easy, but the more support you have, the more likely you'll be to succeed. Others can help us not only try something new but also see it through. My son runs track, and I always find it interesting that as kids come around the final stretch, people start to yell their names, which seems to propel them to run just a little bit faster and a little more confidently to the finish. We all need that support. (And if you don't have a strong network of support, come join the SPL community. We're all about encouragement and building one another up!)

Early on, after I started Simple Purposeful Living, I faced some naysayers. I heard things like, "Your product is too expensive," and encountered people who didn't see my potential. For a time, I allowed those voices to occupy the front row of my life, drowning out the people who truly wanted to cheer me on—like Scott, my sister, Ellen, and my parents. The critics didn't deserve that place, but I let what they had to say linger too long in my head.

It's easy to let the wrong voices take up space in our minds, but we need to be intentional about who gets a front-row seat. Look for people eager to pick up their pom-poms for you—those who see your potential and genuinely want to see you succeed. Those

TINY TWEAKS TO FLEX YOUR FEAR MUSCLE

To set yourself up for success, remember that anticipation is worse than reality and the first time is the hardest, but it'll feel even easier when you have a few successes. Test these tips that have helped me strengthen my fear muscle and try new things.

TINY TWEAK: ASK YOURSELF **TWO QUESTIONS**

We can ask two questions when facing our fears: "What's the worst that can happen?" and "What's the best that can happen?"[2] We often focus on the first question. If you're anything like me, you might be afraid of not nailing the tweak right out of the gate, you might be afraid of what other people say, or you might be afraid you'll try the tweak and it won't work, wasting your time. For example, what's the worst that will happen if I try meal planning? Maybe I'll waste my time, spend extra money, or waste food in the process.

But what's the *best* that could happen if I try meal planning? I'll have a plan for a week's worth of dinners, save money, simplify my life, waste less food, and keep my sanity intact when everyone is hangry.

At the end of the day, what's the likelihood that the worst will happen? And if it does, will you be okay? Even if meal planning doesn't go perfectly in week one, you'll probably learn something from it because, as we've already touched on, failure is a great teacher. And you'll be fine—maybe a little frazzled because you had to run to the store a few times, but you'll be okay.

On the flip side, what if the best happens? Will you be glad you faced your fears and tried? I predict you'll feel proud, confident . . . even transformed.

TINY TWEAK: VISUALIZE SUCCESS

When I was standing on the top of that ski mountain, preparing to race down, I was imagining the worst instead of visualizing success. By vividly imagining yourself walking through what you're afraid to do, you can cultivate confidence, reduce anxiety, and enhance performance. It's like a mental dress rehearsal that prepares individuals to handle potential obstacles and setbacks within the feared scenario. Moreover, it can help you take the first step toward confronting your fears and achieving your goals. With regular practice, visualization becomes a valuable asset in personal development.

Do you want to show up to your day on purpose with a good morning routine? Rehearse what that will look like in your mind. What will you need? Where will you be? It may seem silly to mentally picture yourself in front of the sink with a lineup of face wash, lotion, toothbrush, and toothpaste, but this will help you prepare yourself for success and achieve it, making it a little less scary and a little easier to step into.

TINY TWEAK: HAVE A DEADLINE

The accountability of a deadline for any new skill-building effort or goal will help you make progress and step into your fear. I wanted to run a 5K for years but always stopped short of my goal. I couldn't quite get past running two miles until I signed up for the Turkey Trot at Thanksgiving. The event served as a deadline—I *had* to be ready to run the 5K on Thanksgiving Day. While I wasn't the fastest trotter on the course, that deadline motivated me, setting me up for success. My mom once told me, "If you wait for the timing to be 'just right,' you'll never do anything." Set yourself up for success by giving yourself a deadline and get to work.

TINY TWEAK: GET YOURSELF A HYPE SONG

Jock jams play as the lights dim and flames shoot from the torches. The home team runs onto the floor to the thunderous applause of their fans. How cool would that be? I am adding a moment like that to my bucket list because I'm pretty sure that would hype me up to win the game. What about you? Can we channel that idea and create our own hype songs for key moments in our lives? I did, and it helped so much. It totally set me up for success.

When I started my business, I chose "Fight Song" by Rachel Platten.[3] When my girls started competitive dance, we began to listen to the song "Man! I Feel Like a Woman!" by Shania Twain[4] on the way to every competition. I chose "Brave" by Sara Bareilles[5] when I started writing this book. Another favorite is "Feel This Moment" featuring Christina Aguilera.[6] I danced my way into my forties to that song. Find a good song, put on your headphones like those pro athletes, and hype yourself up. When I dance to my favorite music, I feel the fear melt away as endorphins flood my body,[7] lifting my spirits and filling me with an energy that turns uncertainty into a readiness to tackle anything. And if you need a hype song, borrow one of mine. It's amazing what a little music can do to pump you up!

are the ones you want in your stands, shouting, "You can do it!" as you flex your fear muscle. There's room for more at the table, but make sure those prime seats are filled with voices that uplift and encourage you.

Often, when we try a tweak or step into our fears, we experience setbacks. We take two steps forward and one step back. Failure will make us question our efforts. That's exactly when we need someone to remind us that progress is still being made. So who are your people with pom-poms? How can they help you flex your fear muscle and grow in confidence as you seek the life you long for?

PRACTICE MAKES **PROGRESS**

Smoke billowed up from the roaster as we walked into the house after the Easter service. I was six months pregnant and hosting both of our families for the first time. I should have learned from Clark Griswold how these things go. I burst into tears as I removed the roaster lid to find my Easter ham was now a briquette. My husband and mom saw my distress, ran to the only open store, and brought home pressed canned ham.

I served pressed ham at my first major family function. What a failure . . . or was it?

Babe Ruth was known for saying, "Every strike brings me closer to the next home run."[8] My overcooked ham was a huge swing-and-a-miss, but I was closer than ever to my hosting home run, because I learned a few things from that debacle. First, moments that go sideways make funny and relatable stories later on. Next, never use a brand-new-to-you appliance for the first time at a family function. Finally, food is just the conduit to connection, so it's okay if you serve pressed ham (although I've never needed to since that fateful day).

I wish I could say that was my last kitchen screwup, but a few years later while making a pot of tortellini soup, I learned there's an important distinction between a bulb of garlic and a clove of garlic. The recipe called for garlic, but five *bulbs* of garlic differ from five *cloves* of garlic. I gained a very important culinary lesson from that experience, as a really big pot of tortellini soup went down the drain.

I could have let these screwups keep me from the kitchen entirely. But I didn't want a fear of the stove to shut me down from developing in this area. So I learned to cook the basics. I kept trying new recipes, new techniques. Even though cooking was not a natural talent of mine, I could learn from my failures and keep making progress.

Alison Lumbatis,[9] a guest on my *Simple Purposeful Living* podcast, helps people find their fashion style. During our episode, she said many women she encounters believe they're not fashionable and are afraid of putting together fresh or daring outfits for fear of standing out or creating something that clashes. Unfortunately, too many women internalize these beliefs, even if they're false. But Alison reminded us that fashion is a skill, so just like with cooking, we can hone that skill and learn to put outfits together that work well and suit our shape and personality. Alison urged listeners to start seeing themselves as fashionable women and challenge their ideas about themselves. Confronting what we think applies to more than just fashion.[10]

Don't believe you're organized? Afraid to attempt it for fear you'll devolve back into an out-of-control home overrun by messy piles? It's a skill you can learn. We've all watched organizing shows on TV and felt inspired by the transformation. We run to the store to buy all the supplies we saw the professional organizers haul into the house, sorting items into boxes and file folders, running a few things to a donation box, and completing the project . . . only to find that we aren't any more organized a few weeks later. How deflating. Our failed efforts could create an insurmountable fear response, holding us back from trying again. Before you let fear shut you down, ask yourself: *Did I learn something in the organizing process? Why isn't it working? What did work? How can I tweak it to make it easier to maintain?*

Are you uncomfortable meeting new people? Guess what: You can flex your fear muscle and get more comfortable with that skill. I was incredibly shy as a child. I clung to my mom's leg, bawling on the first day of kindergarten. People who meet me today can't believe I was so shy, but I moved every two years while growing up, which required me to put myself out there and flex my fear muscle to make new friends continually. One move, a kid said, "Are you snobby or just shy?" At that moment, I decided to practice not being shy. We often tell ourselves that we're just not good at (fill in the blank), but many things in our life can be learned, and with practice, we can make progress if we're willing to flex our fear muscle and try.

What's something you believe about yourself? You're not a good cook? You're not a runner? You're not a good friend? You're not organized? What if you could allow yourself the grace to be a beginner and learn to be better at it by flexing your fear muscle and trying?

COURAGE IS BUILT THROUGH TINY ACTS OF BRAVERY THAT FLEX YOUR FEAR MUSCLE.

COURAGE IS CONTAGIOUS

For any of the tweaks in this book to work, no matter how big or small, you must be willing to flex your fear muscle and make a change. Change can be difficult, but kids, colleagues, neighbors, and friends are watching you, finding inspiration as they witness you stepping out of your comfort zone. Flexing your fear muscle has a ripple effect. Courage begets courage. Next time we encourage our middle schooler to memorize their locker combination, our colleague to ask for a raise, our neighbor to contribute to a neighborhood block party, or our friend to host a book club, they have our example to see and know it's possible for them to step up and step out, facing their fears. When we face our fears, we build resilience and confidence and, ultimately, grow into the person we desire to be. We don't grow standing still, sitting in our comfort zone. We grow when we step into fear and try new things.

Courage begets courage.

If you question whether you have what it takes, I see you. You've overcome a lot. You've flexed your fear muscle in the past, and now I am pointing it out to you so you can be more intentional going forward. When anyone in my family faces a challenge, we all repeat: "Flex your fear muscle." You picked up this book because you know we each have only one life, and you want to simplify so you can focus on what matters most, but *that's going to require some changes*. It's time to flex that fear muscle.

Years after that ski race debacle, I signed up for a race similar to the one I'd skipped. As before, I felt my heart rate quicken, my tummy rumble, and my palms sweat as I entered the gate. This time, however, I remembered that sting of regret. My fear muscle was far stronger than it once was, so I took a minute to imagine myself doing the run flawlessly. Then I flexed my fear muscle and skied down the mountain. My mom was at the base of the run with her camera to snap a photo of a smiling girl with her pin and a victorious smile. I was on top of the world physically and emotionally, triumphing over my fears.

We get stronger and braver every time we flex that fear muscle. That's why the tweaks I am offering in this book are minor: You get to flex often but without feeling overwhelmed. I want you to get comfortable trying with the least resistance possible. I'm not asking you to train for a marathon to change your life; I'm asking you to do very simple things. This is a way to set yourself up for success. Even if it's hard and scary, you can face your fears and accomplish your goals if you find ways that are initially simple, small, and doable.

Now that we've laid the groundwork by understanding what brings us joy and how tiny tweaks can lead to big changes, it's time to take action. We made the effort to get our mindset right so we'd be ready to race. In part 2, we're going to clear the clutter, ditch digital distractions, and reclaim our time. We'll focus on planning and automating what truly matters so that we can show up to our day—and our life—on purpose. It's time to push out of the gate, knowing what matters, and fly. Are you ready? Let's do this, sister. I'll grab my pom-poms and cheer you on!

12 TEENY-TINY ACTIONS TO OVERCOME TEENY-TINY FEARS

1. Make a phone call to schedule a medical appointment.
2. Say hi to someone new.
3. Try a new food or recipe.
4. Share your thoughts in a group conversation.
5. Send a text message to someone you haven't talked to in a while.
6. Try a new exercise or workout class.
7. Say no to a request you don't have time for.
8. Ask a question for clarification when you don't understand something.
9. Ask for help when you need it.
10. Make eye contact and smile at strangers.
11. Invite someone to join you for a meal, coffee, or a walk.
12. Ask for forgiveness if you've hurt someone.

Engaging with teeny-tiny fears may seem silly, but facing them can help us gain confidence, be braver, and face bigger fears over time. How can you take a tiny action to face a tiny fear consistently and see how that tiny tweak can radically change your life?

Part 2
Minimize to Maximize

5

CLEAR THE CLUTTER

When I was a little girl, I'd run out to my mailbox each month to see if my *Highlights* magazine had arrived. As soon as it did, I'd race inside, rip open the plastic wrap, and flip straight to the "Hidden Pictures" page—my favorite activity. I'd spend hours hunting for the objects buried in the visual clutter: a baseball bat in place of a zebra's leg, a ball of yarn on a turtle's back. The thrill of finding those tiny, hidden details made me smile victoriously every time.

Fast-forward to the day I was excited to bake chocolate chip banana bread with my kids—the recipe I had tweaked to perfection. Everything was ready, but when I went to grab the spatula from my kitchen drawer, I was met with resistance. The drawer was so overstuffed that I had to wrestle it open, only to poke myself on a skewer I hadn't used in years. What should have been a simple task turned into a frustrating ordeal, and by the time the bread was in the oven, I wasn't just frustrated, I was annoyed, sucking my injured pinkie.

That's the thing about clutter. When our homes are filled with things that don't have a purpose or place, even the simplest tasks feel hard, like hunting for that ball of yarn hidden on the turtle's back. But instead of the joy of the Hidden Pictures pages of my youth, the clutter in real life brings frustration, stress, and lost time.

When our homes are filled with things that don't have a purpose or place, even the simplest tasks feel hard.

Clutter isn't just physical; it's emotional and mental too. The extra stuff we accumulate can steal our peace and add unnecessary stress to our lives. When our spaces are stressful, we internalize that stress, even if we don't realize it. Have you ever come home from a long day to a house full of things all over the place, and all you can see is more work for you to do, another task for you to manage? Maybe you sigh in despair and just turn off the light to that room. Clutter has a way of shutting us down, adding to our mental load, and putting us under the yoke of "I'll never catch up." But it doesn't have to be this way. With a few minor tweaks, we can create spaces that are easy to manage, freeing ourselves from overwhelm and making room for the things that truly matter: joy, peace, and fulfillment.

WHAT IS **CLUTTER**?

Clutter is more than just the physical stuff filling up your home; it's anything that distracts you from living the life you want. It's the buildup of unnecessary, or even necessary, items that don't have a designated place or purpose and begin to crowd your physical and mental space. Clutter can be the extra shoes at the door, piles of paperwork on the counter, or even the sentimental items you've inherited but don't know what to do with. Over time, these things accumulate, making everyday tasks more difficult and adding to your stress. Who wants to cook dinner when you need to clear off the counter first?

Many of us didn't grow up learning how to declutter, and that's not because something was missed. It's because life has changed dramatically over the past several generations. In the past, homes were smaller, and people owned way fewer things. I was reminded of this when I visited a local museum showcasing life from a century ago. We peeked inside the tiny, shallow closet as the docent explained that families stored just a few outfits on hooks—a stark contrast to today's overstuffed closets.

So much has changed in the past hundred years. The Industrial Revolution made mass production possible, and consumerism skyrocketed as people gained more access to affordable goods. Then came the rise of advertising, encouraging us to buy more than we need. Add to that the convenience of online shopping in recent decades, and we find ourselves in homes overflowing with stuff. Today the average American home contains over three hundred thousand items,[1] and we've never had more to manage than we do now. We're managing not only our own belongings but often those we've inherited from previous generations. It's no wonder we feel overwhelmed. But here's the good news: We don't have to feel buried under the weight of

We don't have to feel buried under the weight of our things.

our things. As Marie Kondo famously said, "The question of what you want to own is actually the question of how you want to live."[2]

How do you want to live? Do you want to live more simply, free from your things? Decluttering will help you regain your space and peace of mind.

WHERE TO **START** WITH **DECLUTTERING**?

Now that you understand what clutter is and how we got here, it's time to figure out where to begin. Clutter can come from two primary sources: the everyday items you use but don't have a designated home for, and the excess stuff that's no longer serving you but is still taking up space. The shoes at the door, library books on the couch, and toys scattered around the living room—all are examples of necessary items that can quickly become clutter if left unchecked. If it's necessary but not put away, it's clutter. Meanwhile, that overstuffed closet or jam-packed drawer might indicate excess that needs to be decluttered.

Have you ever noticed clutter acts like a magnet? One pair of shoes by the back door can suddenly multiply into ten, and those small piles on the counter can take over the surface before you know it. The good news? A few minor tweaks can help you manage what you need before it becomes more clutter.

Clutter acts like a magnet. Small piles on the counter can take over the surface before you know it.

TINY TWEAK: ASSIGN HOMES FOR EVERYDAY ITEMS

Remember those library books on the couch? I realized they didn't have a permanent home, so the couch became their default spot. I tweaked this by grabbing a little wire basket from the back room and putting it next to the couch. Now the books have a home, saving me from library fines, and they're easy to access for cozy reading time. Plus, putting them away is a breeze for everyone.

What about your space? Is there something in your home that doesn't have a proper place and ends up adding to the clutter? Look around and choose one item you use daily. Can you give it a permanent home that's easy to access and that everyone in the household knows about? The goal is to make sure you're not the only one putting things away. When everyone knows where things go, you're not the only clutter-culler in the house (say that ten times fast!).

TINY TWEAK: ONE-MINUTE RULE

Shoes by the back door used to pile up, and while that would make a great booby trap for intruders, the pile got *me* every time I came in with bags of groceries. We tried keeping shoes in bedroom closets (because that's what I thought everyone else did?), but no one ever put them away, so I made a tweak: I put a basket for each kid by the back door. Now everyone knows where to put their shoes, at least in theory. When I yell (I mean, *politely remind*), "Put your shoes away," it takes them less than a minute.

The same rule applies to other clutter: If it takes a minute or less to put something away, do it now. This small action prevents clutter from building up and saves you from long tidying sessions later. Whether it's a stray sock, paperwork on the counter, or mail that needs to be recycled (just remove me from the list already), take a moment to put it where it belongs. It makes a big difference.

Glance around your space. Is something sitting out that could be put away in less than a minute? Run and do it! See how good it feels to stop clutter from piling up? It's a buzz rather than a buzzkill later!

STOP CLUTTER BEFORE IT STARTS

We can cut the clutter—even the stuff we need—by building a daily habit of stopping it before it becomes clutter in the first place. Try a little nightly pickup routine before everyone goes to bed. Get into the habit of tidying in transition, like a quick sweep for the two or three items left on a chair or the couch before you put on your pj's and brush your teeth. Alert each person to what you spotted so they take their things to their room, and in theory (because, *kids!*), they'll put them away. "Hey, Quincy, your socks are on the coffee table, and your markers are on the floor, Lucille. Solon and Vera, your laundry is ready to be put away. Can you grab those piles and take them to your room?" These small efforts will make your mornings a little easier. By getting your whole household into the regular rhythm of stowing away necessary items and decluttering a little every day, it will help to keep the overwhelm away.

We can cut the clutter by stopping it before it becomes clutter in the first place.

Stopping the clutter before it starts also helps avoid the shame that clutter will pile on. The more you put it off, the more mental energy it takes up. Clutter isn't kind. It's like little weeds that keep sprouting up all over your house. Taking care of a weed when it's tiny is much easier than when it's big. The same goes for clutter. Deal with it while it's small, and you won't waste time thinking about it later.

TWEAKS TO **CLEAR AWAY** THE **EXCESS**

Now that you've tackled the *necessary* clutter—the stuff you need that was just out of place—it's time to focus on the excess that makes your home feel crowded. In today's world, it's easy for things to accumulate. And it's normal to feel overwhelmed by the clutter. You're not alone.

I met Twyla at a speaking event. She was in her mid-seventies, with a joyful smile and beautiful white hair. Twyla bravely raised her hand after my presentation and shared how overwhelmed she felt by the excess in her home. With her and her husband's health on the decline, she wanted to declutter so it wouldn't all fall on her kids someday, but she didn't know where to start. I could see the weight she was carrying, so I sat down next to her and hugged her.

I told her to think of decluttering as a series of small, manageable steps. How do you climb a mountain? One step at a time. And she did it, one category, one item at a time, with me coaching her through it. We moved through the overwhelm, and you can too. By making these tiny tweaks, you can steadily make progress without feeling overwhelmed.

Step 1: Identify Your Clutter Pain Points

Begin by asking yourself:

- *What areas of my home do I avoid because they're too cluttered?*
- *Which spaces cause me the most stress or frustration?*
- *Where do I waste the most time searching for things?*

Make a list of these trouble spots. Instead of overwhelming yourself with broad categories like "kitchen," break it down into smaller, manageable locations and tasks such as organizing a junk drawer or clearing out a pantry shelf.

For example, Twyla's trouble spot was her office. We broke the larger area down into smaller, specific areas, with a list that looked like this:

- Desk
  - Top of desk
  - Top drawer
  - Middle drawer
- Filing cabinet
- Office fabric shelf
- Closet
  - Top shelf
  - Closet rod
  - Boxes

With this focused plan of attack, Twyla didn't have to panic over decluttering her entire home. She could focus on one manageable area at a time.

Step 2: Start Small and Build Your Confidence

Choose one small area from your list, such as a desk drawer or a cabinet. Twyla chose her desk to have a clear space to work on—smart thinking. Tackling a tiny space first helps build confidence and momentum. I also told Twyla to take a "before" photo of the area because it can be incredibly motivating. This visual record will show how much you've accomplished and inspire you as you move forward. You can send these via text to a supportive friend or family member or post on social media. I love a good "before and progress" photo. Since Twyla didn't have social media, she emailed me her pictures to document her progress. She tackled the top of her desk first and then moved on to the drawers.

Step 3: Keep the Decluttering Process Simple

To keep things organized, use just a few tools: two boxes and a trash bag. Label and use them as follows:

Box #1: Keep but relocate. For items you want to keep but that don't belong in the room you're decluttering.
Box #2: Donate. For items in good condition that you no longer need.
Bag: Trash. For items that need to be thrown away.

Move these containers from room to room as you declutter, relocate items you need to their new or true home, donate what's no longer needed, and toss the trash. Twyla and her husband took the donation boxes to the thrift store weekly, which kept her motivated and helped clear the space for more decluttering. Lean on and ask for support in your own life—whether it's from family, friends, or a support group.

Step 4: Establish Boundaries

Twyla had always cherished her rubber stamp collection, but it had grown so big over the years that it became difficult to find the stamps she truly loved. After some intentional decluttering, she kept only the stamps she really enjoyed, and now she can easily see what she has when she uses the stamps to make cards. She even left a little room for her collection to grow if she finds a stamp she can't resist. By setting boundaries, Twyla was able to create an organized, functional space filled with things she truly loves.

And that's the key—setting clear boundaries for your space. Instead of constantly searching for more storage or new organizing tools, focus on maximizing what you already have. Assign specific spots for your belongings and resist the temptation to fill every nook and cranny. It's okay to leave a little space for your items to shine; that way, it's easier to grab what you need. It's not about the size of your space but how you use it that really counts. I've heard this sentiment said various ways many times: "Instead of focusing on having less, focus on having what you love."

Step 5: Celebrate Your Progress

Remember the story of the tortoise and the hare? Who won the race? That slow and steady tortoise. Be the tortoise and you'll win the decluttering race. Each tiny bit of progress, little tweak by little tweak, adds to significant change. I loved cheering Twyla on as she sent me in-progress shots and updates. If you need someone to cheer you on, tag @simplepurposefulliving on Instagram. I'm here to support you every step of the way. Let's tackle this together and make your home a place of calm and joy.

Clearing the clutter opens up space for happiness to thrive.

TWEAKS FOR WHEN YOU GET STUCK

One day Twyla emailed me and shared how she got completely stuck while going through old photos. The joy of revisiting cherished memories was mixed with the heartache of loss, especially since some family members had passed on. We all hit those moments when we get stuck during the decluttering process. It's not a matter of *if* but *when*.

I could relate all too well. Not only did I have two big boxes of photos in the basement I'd avoided at all costs, but I also had four life-size faux fur sheep my grandmother had gifted me. These sheep, which took up a quarter of my garage, reminded me of the joy and love she poured into our visits. When we would visit her, they would be in the front yard adorned with balloons. I felt a deep connection to them. Letting them go felt like letting go of her love and those happy moments. But when I found a sheep farmer who could appreciate and care for them, I realized that while I was parting with the physical items, the memories and the love remained intact.

Letting go of an item doesn't mean letting go of the memory.

It's important to understand that letting go of an item doesn't mean letting go of the memory. As Francine Jay wisely reminded us, "Your memories are not in your things. The important moments in your life reside in your heart and mind."[3] If you find yourself struggling with letting go of items, the tiniest tweaks, like setting a timer, having a deadline, or seeking support, can make a big difference in getting unstuck. Remember, you don't have to tackle everything at once. Start small and let these tweaks help you maintain momentum toward creating a space that brings you joy.

MAINTAIN THE **MOMENTUM**: THE **DECLUTTER BIN** TWEAK

"There's still more to be done in this room," Twyla wrote, "but I feel like I have accomplished a lot this summer!" I quickly responded that I was proud of her. Bit by bit, she was taking control of the clutter that had once overwhelmed her. Her demeanor had changed, and each email reflected zeal and joy. I cheered her on and suggested her next tweak: a declutter bin to help her maintain momentum.

Here's how it works: Keep a declutter bin handy in your home. It's nothing fancy. Any cardboard box will do. I like to keep ours in the garage, out of sight but easy to access. As you notice things you no longer need or want, toss them into the bin. The other day, Lucille emerged from getting dressed and held out an outgrown shirt. We put it in the bin. The declutter bin keeps things like that shirt from sitting on the counter, where it becomes nagging clutter while waiting to go to the donation center. Worse yet, we may accidentally return it to the closet, where it will take up valuable space until she brings it out again to be donated. When the bin gets full, take it to the donation center or recycle the items.

The hardest part is getting started, but now, like Twyla, you've seen the fruits of your labor. The declutter bin is a simple tweak that makes decluttering a natural part of your routine. Just like a daily reset helps clear necessary clutter, the declutter bin helps tackle the excess. When that free water bottle comes in that you know you'll never use—declutter bin. That pair of shoes your son outgrew—declutter bin. Keep adding to it as you decorate for the seasons or tidy up after holidays. It's all about creating a habit of letting go, one small action at a time. Just like Twyla, you can tweak your way to a clutter-free home and feel happier in the process.

BUT SURELY **I'LL BE HAPPIER** WITH . . .

When I was twelve, I saved up all my money for a pair of Adidas Sambas. My mom wouldn't buy them for me because she didn't understand why I needed soccer shoes if I didn't play soccer. Looking back, I see that she had a point, but at the time I was convinced they were the key to my happiness. I coveted those shoes, dreaming of the day I'd pull them on and lace them up—not to step onto the soccer field but to walk down the halls of my middle school. But the minute I pulled the wadded-up cash from my pleather purse and walked out of Shoe Carnival with the box under my arm, something unexpected happened—the allure of the purchase quickly faded. I learned that the thrill of the hunt was almost more exciting than the actual purchase—how strange! Within days, I started to covet and save for something else; the "happiness" I felt at that moment was already waning.

I'll never forget the day as an adult when I took a load to Goodwill after another closet decluttering session. At one point, I had desperately needed each item in the bag, or so I'd thought, and now they were all being discarded. As I sorted through my donations, I spotted a pair of Sambas in a big bin—someone else had discarded them, like I had. That moment was a powerful reminder of how fleeting the happiness from material things truly is. It was then that I began to understand the cycle I was trapped in—one that left me feeling burdened rather than fulfilled. This realization forced me to confront a deeper issue: my mindset about what I bring into my home. I became more intentional with my purchases when I stopped to realize my motives. Yes, I still buy things—I still love a good purse—but my mindset has shifted. I now know that buying something won't bring lasting happiness. It might serve me, clothe me, or add to my home, but it won't provide true, enduring joy.

Accumulating more things for the sake of happiness does not lead to true joy.

It's easy to forget this when we scroll through social media, watching our favorite influencers share their latest Amazon hauls. We click Buy, not wanting to be left out, thinking this new purchase will make us happy. But here's the truth: The fear of missing out is real, and advertising, peer pressure, and the American way of life convince us that more things will bring more happiness.

From my experience—along with that fateful day when I saw those discarded Sambas—I've discovered the opposite to be true: Accumulating more things for the sake of happiness does not lead to true joy. In fact, it only adds to the clutter that eventually drains us and leaves us feeling overwhelmed. When I am about to make a decision, I use the Cut the Clutter Checklist (see page 86) to help me be more intentional about what I am buying—and *why*—ensuring that I can cut the clutter before it enters our home.

A **DECLUTTERED HOME** IS A PLACE TO **ESCAPE** TO

When we got home from our spring break vacation and unpacked (because I'm one of those people), my husband flopped onto the couch and sighed. "There's no place like home," he said. I sat beside him and leaned my head back, agreeing completely. As you know, I used to love those Hidden Pictures puzzles in my *Highlights* magazine as a kid, but these days, I much prefer a space where everything we love is visible and accessible rather than hidden behind piles of clutter or stuffed in a closet. It's much easier to do what I need to do—and want to do—that way.

Later that day I got off the couch and called the kids, and we made some banana bread. No jammed drawer, all happy smiles. Well, until the mixer got turned too high, but the good news is that with the clutter cleared, it wasn't too hard to clean up.

Moments like these remind me why decluttering matters. Our homes were designed to shelter us from the storm, to be places of refuge. But decluttering isn't just about tidying up; it's about simplifying our space to bring calm, lighten our mental load, and make more room for what we enjoy. Picture a home where the counters are clear, the dining table showcases a single, beautiful centerpiece, and a cozy blanket is ready on the couch. That's a home that welcomes you, not one that adds to your stress.

Our homes were designed to shelter us from the storm, to be places of refuge.

Twyla's story is a perfect example of this. She emailed me to say she uncovered her mom's dishes and a few doilies in her office

TINY TWEAK: CUT THE CLUTTER CHECKLIST

By being intentional with your purchases and using the Cut the Clutter Checklist, you can manage the constant flow of items into your home and stay on top of the clutter.

- **Where will it live?** Ask yourself where you will store this item. Does it have a designated spot in your home? If not, is it worth making a home for?
- **Wait twenty-four hours.** Let it sit in the online shopping cart. Give yourself a day to let the impulse pass. See if you still feel the same way about the item after the initial excitement fades.
- **Heck yes or no?** Be ruthless. If it's not a resounding "Heck yes!" it's a no. This helps prevent unnecessary clutter from sneaking in.
- **Is it really necessary?** Reflect on whether this item truly adds value to your life or if it's just another impulse buy. Consider if it will replace something worn out or if it has a valid reason for being added to your space.

closet and displayed them in her dining room hutch. She said it was a touching reminder of her mom's love every time she walked by. Her story shows that decluttering isn't all about getting rid of things but about making space for what we cherish to shine.

Decluttering isn't all about getting rid of things but about making space for what we cherish to shine.

Decluttering sets the stage for happiness, memory making, and rest. It's not about perfection but about making daily life easier to enjoy. My hope is that, as was the case with Twyla, decluttering helps you create more space for happiness in this one beautiful life you have.

Now that we've made room for joy in our physical spaces, it's time to tackle another source of stress—the kind that's buzzing in your pocket or lighting up your screen. In the next chapter, we'll take a peek at how to ditch those digital distractions and reclaim even more peace in your day.

10 TEENY-TINY THINGS TO DECLUTTER TODAY

Decluttering teeny-tiny things might seem pointless. What difference will one clean counter make when the entire kitchen is in disarray? You know by now that by tackling small items, you build momentum and create a sense of accomplishment. Choose one to tweak today:

1. Kitchen counter
2. Sink full of dishes
3. Top of bedside table
4. Bathroom counter
5. Junk mail, magazines, and newspapers
6. Single socks without a match
7. Unmatched food-storage containers or lids
8. Excess plastic and reusable bags
9. Your purse
10. Makeup and beauty products you never use

6

DITCH THE DIGITAL DISTRACTIONS

Four hours and fifty-seven minutes. The number haunted me. I'd been standing in church singing a worship song, as I tend to be doing every time my Apple Watch buzzes with my weekly screen time report. This time, the alert caught my attention. I had averaged four hours and fifty-seven minutes *per day* last week. I inwardly groaned and rolled my eyes. There was no way I had spent that much time on my phone.

Standing there, I couldn't help but recall a moment from a bloggers' conference I had attended back in 2018. As we sat around tables, we were asked to raise our hands for different amounts of screen time. I distinctly remember being *soooo* proud that I was on the lower end of the spectrum—at around two hours a day. One blogger shared that they spent nearly five hours on their phone daily, and I remember being shocked. I couldn't imagine spending that much time staring at a screen. What do they say? Pride comes before the fall. Mm-hmm.

Here I was a few years later—almost five hours! The very thing that had once surprised me had now become my reality. Sure, I could justify that I ran a small business requiring an online presence, but posting a few stories didn't call for nearly five hours of screen time. And I could justify the Marco Polo updates with my sister, Ellen, halfway around the world, but deep down, I knew the problem wasn't my phone—it was me.

That number—four hours and fifty-seven minutes—added up to over one thousand eight hundred hours in a year. To put it into perspective, that's *seventy-six full days* per year looking at my phone alone. If I slept eight hours a night, that means I was spending nearly 30 percent of my waking hours on a screen. To make matters worse, when I stopped to think about it, I wasn't spending that kind of time in person each week with anyone I cared about. *Where was the barf emoji when I needed it?*

Later that day, the realization hit even harder. My daughter Lucille was sitting on the couch, flicking her finger across the blank screen of a toy phone, perfectly imitating what she'd seen me do countless times. The phone wasn't even on, but she'd mastered the motion. As I sat next to her, nose deep in my own phone, my kids called out for my attention, and my son bluntly said, "Mom, you always tell us not to be on screens too much, but you're always on your phone."

Ouch. The callout stung. He wasn't wrong. I had fallen into the same trap I once marveled at, letting my phone consume my time without realizing it. And now, my kids were not only noticing but imitating my behavior.

ADDRESSING **DIGITAL DISTRACTIONS**

When we're tweaking our way to a simplified life and looking to reclaim more minutes for happiness and joy, we must address the digital distractions pulling us away. The minutes are right there, buzzing in our pockets.

It's not only me. The world has shifted, and we're all spending more and more time glued to our devices. The average American now spends four hours and thirty minutes a day on their phones, and globally, we check our phones around ninety-six times a day.[1]

While technology has made many aspects of life easier, it has also created new challenges. Apps and platforms are designed to engage us, offering endless content, notifications, and connections that keep us coming back for more. And let's be honest—it's easy to fall into these habits, especially when the dopamine hit from a notification or a Like feels rewarding.[2]

> The real issue isn't the apps—it's how we choose to use them.

But the real issue isn't the apps—it's how we choose to use them. Little by little, our habits have shifted with technology advances, and for many of us, our phones have started consuming hours of our days. For me, that number—four hours and fifty-seven minutes—was a wake-up call. I didn't want to look back in another five years and realize I was spending even more time on my phone. It was ample motivation to make some tweaks so my life could flourish with what truly mattered—the things I know bring true happiness.

HOW **HABITS** TAKE OVER

A few years ago we laid down new sod in our yard, and at first it looked perfect. But over time, I started to notice weeds creeping in around the edges. Initially, it didn't seem like a big deal—just a few here and there. But little by little, those weeds took over. Soon they were choking out the new grass, and Scott and I spent hours pulling up those weeds. It wasn't enough to lay the sod and walk away; I had to tend to it regularly to keep it healthy.

Technology is a lot like that. It offers helpful features, but if we're not careful and intentional, it creeps in and takes over. The distractions and constant pulls from our devices steal away our time, our focus, and our ability to be present. We don't notice it at first, but little by little, it starts to choke out the important parts of our lives: our family time, our peace, and our moments of joy. Just as a garden doesn't flourish by accident, our time and attention don't either.

TWEAKING OUR WAY TO **INTENTIONALITY**

We can't reject our phones or technology entirely—they're here to stay, and they are an essential part of the way most of us do life. The challenge is learning how to reclaim control over how we use them. By making small, thoughtful tweaks, we can set boundaries, create more intentional habits, and reclaim precious moments of our lives. With those adjustments, we can create space for rest, connection, and joy in a world constantly competing for our attention.

TINY TWEAKS FOR TECH

TINY TWEAK: OPT OUT OF ALL PUSH NOTIFICATIONS

Every app thinks it deserves your attention. But do you need to know every time someone comments or a flash sale hits? The best tiny tweak here is to silence them all. I've limited my notifications to texts, calls, and customer order notifications, because I do a happy dance when one comes through (seriously!), and then I ship them. But everything else? Gone.

Do you often check your phone because of random notifications? If yes, go into Settings right now and turn off notifications. Check, done! Look at you, girl!

TINY TWEAK: USE DO NOT DISTURB

I started using this feature to avoid "dings" during my podcast recordings, and it was a game changer. Now I use it during writing sessions, family time, and even meetings. And here's the best part: You can still customize it to allow important calls (like from your kids or spouse) to get through while silencing everything else.

Do notifications pull you out of conversations or tasks? Try Do Not Disturb to focus better.

TINY TWEAK: LEAVE YOUR DEVICES OUT OF SIGHT

Out of sight, out of mind works. This could mean plugging in your phone in another room during dinner or tossing it into your purse when you're out with friends. Let's be honest: If you don't see it, you're a lot less likely to check it every five minutes.

Are you tempted to check your phone when there's a lull in conversation? Try placing it in a bag or another room to stay in the moment.

TINY TWEAK: SET LIMITS

Numbers don't lie. When I saw my screen time stats, I nearly fainted. You can use tools on your phone to set realistic limits for apps with which you need to set boundaries. I set one for social media, and I try to stay within my daily limit. But when that notification occasionally pops up, it's a helpful nudge to put my phone away. Progress, not perfection, sis!

Do you spend more time on your phone than you'd like to admit? Try setting app limits for most-used apps.

TINY TWEAK: MOVE ALL APPS OFF YOUR HOME SCREEN

This is the tiniest of tweaks, but wow, does it help! Moving apps off your home screen makes it less likely that you'll tap them mindlessly. It prevents the classic "if you give a mouse a cookie" scenario, where you pick up your phone to make a dentist appointment but you see the Instagram app, which leads to twenty minutes lost down the rabbit hole and no appointment made. I can't be the only one.

Do you unlock your phone for one thing and end up doing something else entirely? Move the culprit apps off your home screen.

TINY TWEAK: PICK A TIME TO GO TECH-FREE

One Sunday, I accidentally left my phone at home when we went out to lunch and ran errands—and guess what? I initially freaked out, but my husband had his phone, and not only did I survive but it was also freeing. Sometimes we need a break from tech. Pick an hour, an afternoon, or even a day to unplug and reconnect with real life.

When was the last time you went without your phone for a few hours? Try leaving it behind, especially if you're with someone else who has a phone in case of an emergency.

TINY TWEAK: DELETE APPS FOR A PERIOD

You know I take weekends offline, and when I have decided not to, I have lived to regret it. If you need a deeper break, try temporarily deleting your most-used apps. My mom only downloads her favorite (but addictive—*Candy Crush Saga*) game during long trips, which works like a charm!

Do you feel drained from too much time online? Try unplugging from your most-used apps.

TINY TWEAK: CHOOSE TECH-FREE ZONES

We have a no-tech-table rule for family meals. Tech-free zones, like the dinner table or bedrooms, can help create more meaningful interactions and fewer distractions. Plus, if I slip and bring my phone to the table, my family loves to call me out. Fun times!

Is there a place you want to be fully present and tech-free? Try creating a tech-free zone.

TINY TWEAK: DITCH THE SMARTWATCH

I ditched my Apple Watch after realizing how much the constant notifications fragmented my attention. Remember how those dings can derail your thinking? It seemed that my watch derailed me every five minutes. Research shows even a brief interruption can take up to twenty-three minutes to recover from.[3] So I swapped it out for a simple, non-Bluetooth digital watch and pedometer, and it's been a breath of fresh air.

Do smartwatch notifications distract you from being in the moment? Could taking a break from your watch help you focus?

TINY TWEAK: SET ALARMS FOR FOCUS

Alarms can actually help reduce distractions. Instead of constantly checking the time or worrying about being late, set an alarm to remind yourself when it's time to go. This way, you can stay present without looking at your phone.

Do you constantly check your phone out of fear you'll miss something? Could setting alarms help you stay more focused and present?

TIME TO **UNPLUG**

I spend a lot of time on my phone and social media apps throughout the week for work. By Friday, I often feel like I've been running on fumes. My creativity is at an all-time low, and everything feels like an uphill push. I find myself slipping into comparison mode more easily and not feeling like myself. With all four kids in school, I really cherish our weekend time together, and I don't want to miss out on it because I'm glued to a screen.

For me, the first tweak to ditch the digital distractions was unplugging from social media. It was my biggest "weed" and seemed like the best place to start. I came across a quote from Anne Lamott that I love: "Almost everything will work again if you unplug it for a few minutes, including you."[4] It's always been true for my computer; maybe I should test it on myself? To "unplug," I took the weekends offline. No posts, no stories—just time away. The world would survive without me.

Unplugging can look different for everyone. For me, it meant stepping away from social media. But really, it's about laying down those digital distractions in favor of being present in the moment. It's about creating space where you aren't constantly pulled away by notifications and scrolling, so you can be fully engaged with life right in front of you. But before you can fully "unplug," it's important to first *identify your digital habits*—to figure out what your biggest culprits are.

Take a moment to reflect: What apps or activities consume the most of your time? Are you scrolling through Instagram during lunch breaks, checking emails at the dinner table, or pulling out your phone absentmindedly when you're bored? Tracking your screen time can offer eye-opening insights into where digital distractions, actual habits, sneak in and steal your moments.

What I discovered was that my phone had become an easy button for entertainment. When I was waiting in the checkout line or wanted to escape, I'd absentmindedly pull it out and scroll. But when I put it away, I found that real life offered an even better version of entertainment and escape. Riding bikes with the kids, sitting on the back porch with Scott for Saturday morning coffee, cheering on our favorite sports team with a smorgasbord of appetizers—these experiences were richer, more fulfilling. Sure, it took a little more effort, but in that space, I was more intentional about pursuing those moments. My fear of missing out turned into the *joy* of missing out. My creativity came back, my anxiety dipped, and I walked into the new week feeling refreshed and ready.

My fear of missing out turned into the *joy* of missing out.

Hannah Brencher, author of *The Unplugged Hours*,[5] found something similar when she started intentionally carving out unplugged hours. She set a goal to find one thousand unplugged hours in a year, about three hours daily. She said:

> Hour by hour I was reclaiming my life for things I was passionate about, things I let slip by the wayside. The biggest thing was that I started to see that the connectivity with my devices was fueling the overwhelm. I wanted to live simply and intentionally, and I found that when I powered down my phone, that was within my reach. . . . All the tasks I had on my list, I could do, one task to the

> next task. What was really getting me was the constant flicking . . . from this thing to that thing, this app to that app. My brain was tired, and it couldn't carry the mental load it was expected to hold at that time.[6]

The tweak you need might not be a weekend away from social media. Maybe for you, it's as simple as carving out an hour of screen-free time each day. Studies show that stepping away from technology improves mental health, reduces stress, and fosters greater creativity. When we're not constantly distracted by notifications and endless scrolling, we can be more present, mindful, and connected to the things right in front of us.[7]

To figure out a tweak to start unplugging, here are some questions to ask yourself:

- *Do I feel like I need more time in my day?*
- *What digital habits or apps most often pull me away?*

START SMALL TO DITCH DIGITAL DISTRACTIONS

It's incredible how a single *ding* from your phone can completely derail your train of thought. One moment, you're knee-deep in a project or conversation, and the next, you've forgotten what you were doing—pulled out of the present moment, often without returning to it. Rude, right? If you found yourself saying yes, you want more minutes in your day, or apps are stealing your attention, it doesn't take a massive overhaul to fix it. Let's start small with—you guessed it—tiny tweaks that can help you stay present,

RECLAIM YOUR TIME AND CULTIVATE DEEPER CONNECTIONS.

focused, and more intentional. I've included several Tiny Weaks for Tech in this chapter (see pages 93–96) to get you started.

I know some of these tweaks might not work for you, and that's okay. The goal here isn't to tackle them all—it's to spark some ideas on how a tiny tweak can make a big difference in ditching digital distractions. Take what's helpful and leave the rest. These tweaks are flexible, and the beauty is that you can tailor them to fit your life.

What's one tweak you can start with today? Pick one that speaks to you and give it a try. Even a small adjustment can have a huge impact on how present you feel in your everyday moments. Start small and see where it takes you.

CREATING A **DIGITAL SUNSET**: MY NEXT TWEAK

After starting small with these tiny tweaks, I quickly realized there was one area where my self-control was officially on vacation—probably sipping a piña colada on some far-off beach. There I was, curled up in bed, completely wiped, but instead of resting, I was glued to my phone, mindlessly scrolling through social media. One minute I'd be watching cute dog videos, and the next I'd find myself deep in the profile of someone I didn't even follow, wondering what on earth I was doing with my life. Before I knew it, the clock had ticked past my bedtime, and my beloved book—one that always brings me joy—was left unopened. Worse, I wasn't getting enough sleep, and we all know lack of sleep is a serious thief of joy.

That's when I realized my next tiny tweak had to be setting what productivity and sleep experts call a *digital sunset*.[8] Phones aren't the enemy—no need to throw them into the lake yet. They're

IS A DIGITAL SUNSET RIGHT FOR YOU?

IS YOUR SLEEP AFFECTED BY NIGHTTIME PHONE USE?

If you are scrolling late into the night and sacrificing sleep, unplugging or creating a digital sunset could improve your rest and overall well-being.

DO YOU HAVE TROUBLE DISCONNECTING FROM WORK OR SOCIAL MEDIA IN THE EVENING?

If you're still mentally engaged with work emails or social media before bed, implementing a digital sunset could help create boundaries and give your mind a break from constant input.

a great tool, but like other tools, it's all about how and when you use them. I needed to be smarter about this tool, especially in the evening when my brain was running on empty. If I wanted to reclaim my evenings and get back to reading, sleeping, and, you know, actually resting, I had to make a change.

Enter: my digital sunset. I started putting my phone to bed. Yes, I literally put *it* to sleep before *I* went to sleep. I charged it in our adjacent bathroom, which was close enough for emergencies but far enough that I couldn't grab it and start scrolling. This small tweak wasn't about creating distance; it was about reclaiming my evenings and getting my life (and bedtime) back on track.

After seeing how well the digital sunset worked for me, we decided to invite our kids to adopt the practice too. If it helped me get better sleep and disconnect in a healthier way, surely it could benefit them as well. Now all our phones and devices "go to bed" in the bathroom, giving us time to unwind and connect with one another before heading to sleep.

Here's where the magic happened: As a result of this digital sunset, my big kids started dropping off their phones and "tucking us in." Some nights it's a quick hug, but other nights, they climb into bed and chat for a while. As they age, these conversations mean more and more to me. Who knew that an unintended blessing of the digital sunset would be something that brings me the most joy every single day? What started as a small tweak to reduce screen time has turned into a beautiful time for connection with my kids, something I never could have predicted.

And there's real science behind why this works. Studies show that putting your phone away before bed not only helps with sleep[9] but it also helps with mental clarity, reduces stress, and improves family relationships. The blue light from screens messes with melatonin, our body's sleep hormone, and even quick phone checks can delay your sleep cycle by thirty minutes or more.[10] Plus, having the phone out of reach makes it easier to resist that "just one more scroll" which, let's be real, never ends with one.

This small action creates the space we need to focus on what matters, whether that's more sleep, time with loved ones, or a little peace and quiet at the end of a long day.

With the digital sunset in place, I'm going to bed earlier,

sleeping better, and waking up ready to greet the day—on *my* terms, not my phone's. And best of all, my kids are learning these healthy habits too. It's a win-win all around and an unexpected joy I get to experience every night. I thought I would feel deprived, but I don't at all.

FINDING BALANCE BETWEEN WORK AND DIGITAL DISTRACTIONS

We've talked a lot about setting boundaries with personal phone use, but it's equally important to set healthy boundaries with work—especially now that much of our work is done online. In today's world, it's easy for digital distractions to spill over from social media into work emails and online projects, making it difficult to draw a clear line between work and home life.

Even a good thing, like loving what you do, can become a bad thing when it takes over your life. My family comes from a long line of hard workers, and while that passion for work is a strength, it sometimes means we struggle with balance. When I first started my business, my dad shared his regret about not always balancing work and family well, telling me that kids grow up fast. I took that advice to heart, and I've made it a priority to find healthier ways to balance work and family, even as my work remains heavily tied to digital spaces.

One thing I've learned is that balance is a lot like riding a bike. Sometimes you lean more into work, other times into home life. It's not always perfect, but over time, you find ways to make it work. Acknowledging those shifts, both with yourself and with the people

TWEAKS FOR MANAGING WORK-RELATED DIGITAL DISTRACTIONS

1. **Set clear email boundaries.** If responding to emails on your phone isn't effective, consider deleting the app. Limit checking your inbox to a few scheduled times a day to avoid constant interruptions.
2. **Close the door on work.** If you work from home, physically closing your office door signals the end of your workday and helps you mentally transition from work to family time. When the door closes, leave the work phone on your desk (or at least silence Slack).
3. **Create a buffer time.** Set an alarm for ten minutes before your family gets home to wind down from work mode and prepare to be fully present.
4. **Have a family conversation.** During busy work seasons, communicate openly with your family. Let them know when work needs more of your attention and assure them it's temporary.
5. **Check in with your partner.** Regular check-ins with your spouse or partner can help you stay accountable and balance work and home life.

who matter—your children, your spouse—is crucial to maintaining that balance.

To help limit work-related digital distractions, I've incorporated small tweaks that have made a big difference. For example, I removed email from my phone. Trying to respond on my iPhone often leads to typos or half-finished thoughts, and I found myself reading emails without actually replying. Now I check my email only twice a day—once in the morning and once before the end of my workday—and I close the door to my office when I'm done.

But even with these boundaries in place, there are still seasons when work requires more focus. When that happens, I make sure to communicate with my family, letting them know it's temporary. My kids, now older, even hold me accountable. Checking in with my husband also helps me stay on track and ensures I'm not tipping too far into work mode.

While my tweaks may not work for everyone, they've given me the space to separate work from home life and manage digital distractions more effectively. Hopefully these ideas will spark some thoughts about what boundaries might work best for you.

FROM **DIGITAL** DISTRACTION TO DIGITAL **DILIGENCE**

As I reflect on my digital journey, I'm starting to make real progress with my phone usage. I've become more aware of when I'm pulled to grab my phone, and instead of mindlessly reaching for it, I take a moment to check in with myself. *Why am I reaching for this? Do I want to escape or avoid something?* When I start to feel comparison and discontentment creep in, I know it's time to put my phone down. Comparing my real life to someone else's highlight reel is a recipe for disaster. The truth is, it takes diligence and humility to navigate this space, but here's the thing: Phones are not the enemy. They're only a tool, and we have the power to use them for good in our lives.

Phones are not the enemy. They're only a tool, and we have the power to use them for good in our lives.

As my therapist wisely told me, it's not about hitting a finish line but about focusing on who you are becoming. We can tweak our way to finding a good rhythm with our digital devices. Sure, we might mess up, but mistakes are great teachers, not only for us but also for those who are watching us. We're human, and it's okay for those who look up to us to see that we struggle too. It's through that struggle that we find our way.

With a few intentional tweaks, I've been able to tend to those digital weeds and reclaim some of those lost minutes for the things that truly bring happiness and joy. When my kids ask me to play a game now, I set my phone down without hesitation. I'm learning to choose presence over distraction, and there's a whole lot of grace in that process. The key is to keep checking in with ourselves, keep making small adjustments, and keep moving toward a life filled with more of what truly matters.

And remember what Anne Lamott said: "Almost everything will work again if you unplug it for a few minutes, including you."[11] Sometimes stepping away from the digital noise is all it takes to reset and reconnect with what brings true fulfillment.

YOUR PHONE HAS AN OFF BUTTON: A DIGITAL DETOX

After trying a digital sunset routine, it might be time for a deeper reset—a digital detox. I suggest trying a forty-eight-hour phone break. See if you can not only survive without your phone for a couple of days but also use the detox as an opportunity to reset your habits and make time for things that fill you.

IS A DIGITAL DETOX RIGHT FOR YOU?

Ask yourself:

Do I feel anxious after scrolling?
Is my phone pulling me away from family moments?
Is it disrupting my focus or productivity?

HOW TO CREATE A DIGITAL DETOX THAT WORKS:

- Identify your biggest distraction. Which app or platform drains you the most?
- Start small. Pick a time frame that works for you, like a tech-free evening or weekend.
- Have a plan. Fill your time with things that bring joy: reading, walking, or playing with your kids.

7

MAKE THE MOST OF YOUR MINUTES

I grabbed my phone in its bright-pink case off the kitchen counter and called for the kids as I walked out to the front porch. My ferns were looking a little wilted under the August sun as the kids filed out and groaned in unison, asking if we could make it quick—there were other people outside, after all. *The audacity!* The neighbors were all doing the same thing we were, and I couldn't help but smile. I lined up my kids by age, a natural stairstep, as we had for our annual first-day-of-school photo since our eldest started preschool thirteen years before. Over time, we've added siblings, inches, and memories, but this tiny tradition has remained unchanged.

As they stood there, grinning and bearing it, my daughters were in their carefully chosen outfits, Vera in a red ruched shirt and black shorts, and Lucille in a "Cultivate Love" graphic tee and favorite shorts with her new tennis shoes, which happened to be Adidas Sambas.

(I couldn't *believe* it when she picked them out! Everything that goes around comes around, doesn't it?) And the boys were in whatever they had pulled from their drawers, even though I had offered to buy them a new first-day-of-school outfit. They weren't interested.

I felt a familiar tug at my heart. Every year, this ritual seemed to mark not only the passage of another school year but also how time itself was slipping through my fingers. My elder son, Solon, now stood tall in high school, with just three more first-day photos left before he was off to college. *How did we get here?*

I clicked the camera button, making sure everyone was looking at me and wanting to freeze this moment in time. To somehow capture their smiles and the entire feeling—the laughter, the groans, the anticipation of a new year. But as much as I tried, time moved on, relentless and unstoppable.

It's hard not to feel the sting of time slipping away.

The Facebook memories that popped up that morning didn't help either. Image after image, I saw my kids growing up before my eyes: Solon's chubby baby cheeks giving way to a chiseled jawline, his carefree giggles replaced by a deep voice that still catches me off guard.

It's hard not to feel the sting of time slipping away, especially on days like that. I couldn't help but wonder, *Had I done enough with those years? Had I truly made the most of the moments, or had I let too many of them get lost in the busyness of life?*

I often think about this during the small, everyday moments that end up meaning so much. It feels like time is speeding by, and I'm desperately trying to slow it down, wishing I could hold on to these moments a little longer.

BUT WON'T I BE HAPPIER WITH MORE TIME?

"If only I had a little more time." We've all said it, whether we're on a stoop snapping a photo or we're lamenting that our to-do list feels too long for the hours in the day. We hope more time will magically lead to more happiness, more productivity, and more fulfillment. But here's the reality check: Does more time actually make us happier or more productive?

I used to think so. Whenever I had one of those days when my schedule was blissfully clear, I'd get excited, envisioning everything I'd accomplish. But with all the time in the world, I'd put things off—only to find myself sprawled on the couch, binge-watching Hallmark movies and scrolling my phone, still in my pajamas at 2 p.m. I would find I had frittered away precious hours doing nothing productive, my to-do list gathering dust. Don't get me wrong, there's a time and a place for rest and Hallmark movies, but that moment taught me an important lesson: More time doesn't always mean more happiness or productivity. In fact, without intention, more time can feel overwhelming and directionless.

Without intention, more time can feel overwhelming and directionless.

When I started writing this book, I didn't realize how often we fall into this trap—believing that if we had a little more of something, we'd finally be happy. More money, more followers, more time—it's a mirage. But just like more money doesn't necessarily lead to more happiness, the same goes for time. Cassie Holmes came to this same conclusion in her book, *Happier Hour*.[1] After a grueling workweek, she fantasized about quitting her job and moving to a tropical island—a daydream many of us have entertained. I know I have. I'd be much happier with endless hours sipping on mai tais (yes, like my grandpa) on the beach. But instead of booking that one-way ticket, she dug into the concept of discretionary time and discovered a "sweet spot" for happiness.

What's the sweet spot? Holmes found through her research that two to five hours of discretionary time each day is ideal. She called it discretionary time, but I like to call these moments "Happiness Spaces." To allow for these, we aren't just trimming time for efficiency, but we're intentionally carving out moments for activities that bring us joy and fulfillment—the things that light us up. We want

"HOW YOU SPEND YOUR TIME" AUDIT

Apply what you know. Review how you spend your time and identify how much is dedicated to activities that bring you joy. Remember, these are your Happiness Spaces.

Capitalize on the tweak. Based on your assessment, adjust your schedule to increase your time spent on joy-bringing activities. Aim for that sweet spot of two to five hours of intentional happiness per day, and watch how even small tweaks can lead to a more joyful, fulfilling life.

to leave space for the stuff that matters most, what we wrote down in chapter 3, the things that keep popping up in our gratitude journals. These are the activities that don't just fill our days but truly fulfill us.

In the same way that we discuss white space when decluttering (see page 139), we're deliberately making room in our lives for these Happiness Spaces. By freeing up two to five hours, we can devote that time to hobbies, relaxation, socializing, or anything that brings happiness—even the Hallmark movie binge, but with intention and awareness of why we're sitting there watching.

Just as Twyla's mom's dishes shone on display in her uncluttered hutch, the things we love to do and that bring us joy shine when we create Happiness Spaces. When we intentionally carve out time for what lights us up, those moments stand out, bringing fulfillment to our everyday lives.

When I first read that all you need to be truly happy is two to five hours of these Happiness Spaces per day, I thought, *No way do I have two hours of free time in my day!* But then I decided to audit a random weekday:

- Coffee and my gratitude journal = 15 minutes
- A walk = 30 minutes
- Marco Polo chat with my sister = 15 minutes
- Family dinner = 20 minutes
- Reading with Quincy and Lucille before bed = 20 minutes
- Reading before bed = 15 minutes

That totals 1 hour and 55 minutes of intentional happiness. I was close—five minutes shy of the sweet spot. Turns out I was already spending time on what mattered, even if it was less than I'd like. This little audit helped me understand how to better shape my days and make room for what truly brings me joy.

The truth is, we don't need endless hours to feel content—just a bit of intention and a few small adjustments. We have more power over our time than we think, and by intentionally shaping how we use it, we can transform our days from chaotic to fulfilling.

TRIMMING THE TIME FOR YOUR DAILY TASKS

Whenever I make a to-do list, I'm guilty of sneaking in tasks I've already completed, just to feel that instant gratification of crossing something off. Anyone else? It's like giving yourself a mini victory dance! And hey, since you've already started decluttering your spaces and ditching those digital distractions, you've already crossed off something from the list and reclaimed some minutes for happiness. Go ahead, give yourself a high five!

Now, let's talk about those everyday essentials—the laundry, meal prep, carpooling, work projects. You know, the stuff that's non-negotiable because it helps keep our lives (and our loved ones') running smoothly. This stuff isn't just busywork; it's how we care for our families, our homes, and even ourselves. But even though these tasks are part of what makes life meaningful, they can still feel overwhelming.

The good news? With a few tiny tweaks, we can streamline those must-dos and free up more time for what lights us up. It's not about speeding through life; it's about finding a rhythm that makes room for joy. So let's roll up our sleeves and see where we can trim a few minutes here and there—because those little wins can add up to more Happiness Spaces in your day.

Research shows that when we neglect the activities that bring us joy, our life satisfaction tends to dip.[2] Instead of letting those fun things languish at the bottom of the list, let's flip the script. By simplifying and streamlining the tasks we have to do, we can reclaim those precious minutes and redirect them toward the things that make us happy. Ready to take control and make every minute count? Let's do this!

TIME-TRIMMING **TWEAKS**

Tiny Tweak: Stop, Drop, and Roll

I brought my friend Rachel a hot meal, diapers, and one of our company's signature Brain Dump notepads when she had her fifth baby. Since she was a mom of five, I knew she had all the other essentials, but these items would be lifesavers during her busy days. A few weeks later, she messaged me to say she had tried out the Brain Dump notepad, listing everything she needed and wanted to do between diaper changes, and couldn't believe how much she got done—and in a sensible order. What she thought was an impossible list suddenly became manageable, and she even had time for what she really wanted to do in this season—baby snuggles and some much-needed rest.

Brain dumps streamline our to-do lists, making us more efficient and freeing up precious minutes we can reclaim for things that truly bring us joy. If you catch yourself saying, "I have a lot on my plate," "My mind is racing," or "I can't focus," that's a clear signal to pause

THE D.R.O.P. METHOD
Stop, Drop, and Roll to Unload Your Brain

Dump. Start by writing down everything you need and want to do. This could be anything from showering and taking a walk to doing laundry and calling the gynecologist for your annual exam. The goal here is to empty your brain of every task, big or small, that needs attention. But don't forget to include things you *want* to do as well. Those matter most, so you know what you're aiming for when discretionary moments free up. What gets written down gets done. Make sure you're listing both the essentials and the joy-bringing activities.

Rank and organize. Once everything is listed, it's time to rank and organize. Decide what's most important and urgent, helping you focus your efforts. Remember, not everything will be a top priority. Break it down into must-dos, nice-to-dos, and nonessentials. To effectively prioritize, start with the hardest and most urgent task first—"Eating the frog,"[3] as Brian Tracy popularized in *Eat That Frog!*[4] Getting your toughest task out of the way gives you momentum for the rest of the day.

Purge. Now, review your list. Do you really need to do everything yourself? This is where you can delegate or discard nonessential tasks. It's okay to let some things go. Can your kids unload the dishwasher? Could you get groceries delivered? The key is to delegate or eliminate where possible, to free up your time and energy for both the necessary and the joyful tasks.

and do a brain dump. Your anxious phrases are often signs that mental clutter is taking over, and a brain dump will help clear the fog and make space for what matters.

How did Rachel achieve this magic trick? She stopped, dropped, and rolled. While her hair might have figuratively felt like it was on fire, she took a few moments to brain dump using the D.R.O.P. method (see page 116). By taking this essential step, she was ready to roll with newfound efficiency.

Once you complete the ten-minute D.R.O.P. exercise, you'll have a clear, prioritized itinerary for your day. Focus on the top items on your list—they're the most crucial and will get done first. If you don't end up tackling the less critical tasks, simply move them to another day, delegate them, or let them go.

But don't make a habit of pushing the want-tos to the bottom. Finding a balance between the need-tos and the want-tos is how you move from a functional life to a fulfilling one. The want-tos are what make your day brighter and more fun, adding joy to your routine. Living from your values and including what matters most to you help everything go more smoothly.

I've used this D.R.O.P. method for years, and like my friend Rachel, who used it to handle everything she needed to do—and still had time for baby snuggles—you'll find that your tasks don't take as long as you might expect. This approach eliminates the "What should I do next?" feeling, minimizes distractions, and treats time as a valuable tool, freeing up more minutes than you thought possible. The next time your mind feels cluttered, stop, drop, and roll. It's your first tweak toward maximizing your minutes for what truly matters.

Question: *What's one task you can add to your list today that you want to do but often push to the bottom?*

Tiny Tweak: Monotask

One afternoon, I was trying to get dinner ready before taking my daughter to dance class. I lit the burner for the pasta and left the pot to boil while I helped Lucille with her homework. Quincy saw an opportunity and asked for iPad time. Without thinking it through, I agreed. I finished adding the pasta to the pot and returned to assist Lucille.

Meanwhile, the unattended pot boiled over, and the gas flame was extinguished. As we wrapped up the homework, I started to smell gas. The chaos of the moment led to a mess in the kitchen. The pasta was ruined, and I found myself scolding Quincy for using the iPad—a privilege I had already granted. I thought multitasking would help, but it turned my day into a disaster.

Here's the truth: Multitasking is a myth. We've been conditioned to believe that handling multiple tasks simultaneously is the key to productivity. Yet our brains are actually wired to monotask. When we split our attention, none of the functions receive our complete focus, leading to mistakes and inefficiencies[5] and frozen pizza for dinner because the pasta's ruined.

Tiny Tweak: Make a Dreaded Task Fun

One day, while my dad and I were sitting around the campfire at the lake, he shared a little tweak he'd made to his routine. He had been struggling to make time for rowing on his machine, even though he knew it was important for his health. Then he made a small, simple change. My dad paired his must-do activity—rowing—with something he genuinely enjoyed. He started DVRing the evening news and watching it early the next morning while rowing. Suddenly that dreaded workout became something he looked forward to.

PRACTICE MONOTASKING

Try dedicating your attention to one task at a time. Try being present in the moment, whether enjoying a meal, reading a book, or helping your child with homework. While it's true that our kids can make it challenging to stick to this approach, when we choose to focus on one task at a time, it can improve our ability to handle their questions and be more present. Though it might seem like you're doing less, this approach leads to greater efficiency. Your brain can avoid constantly switching between tasks, which can be mentally exhausting.

Think of monotasking like an assembly line. When the kids help me package up all the SPL notepads, I give each person one part of the process. They either bag it, close it, or sticker it. They get good at that one part rather than flipping back and forth between what they're doing. As each of us concentrates on a specific step, allowing for a smoother and faster packing process, focusing solely on one task at a time streamlines our efforts. Dedicating your full attention to a single task reduces mistakes and completes the task more quickly. Monotasking helps you simplify what you need to do once again, maximizing those precious minutes we want to reserve for more joy and happiness.

This mirrors what Greg McKeown talked about in his book *Effortless*.[6] McKeown suggested that when you pair a task you have to do with something you enjoy, it can make the effort feel lighter. In my dad's case, the news made rowing more enjoyable, turning a must-do into something fun. Multitasking can be your friend when it helps make a dreaded task more enjoyable. While our brains are wired to focus on one thing at a time, pairing a not-so-fun task with something enjoyable allows you to focus on the fun part instead. For instance, I started walking every morning just to catch up on Ellen's Marco Polo updates, and it turned walking into something I looked forward to.

Tiny Tweak: Use Timers for Your Task

I used to dread mopping the floors on Sunday night, because I thought it would take so long and ruin my evening, but I sure did love waking up Monday morning to a tidy house ready for the busy week ahead. Our brains have this funny way of making us think undesirable tasks take forever. Research suggests that we overestimate the time it takes to complete tasks we don't enjoy.[7]

A few years back, I decided to prove my thoughts wrong. I started timing myself mopping the floor as part of our Sunday-night tidy routine. My brain insisted it took an hour, making me dread it even more. But you know what? It only took about ten minutes to mop the main floor—just ten minutes. That's less than 1 percent of my day, let alone my week. Once I realized that, I made it even more fun by creating a cleaning playlist with upbeat music. It's like Zumba meets cleaning. Just call it *zoom-clean*! Have I accidentally invented a new exercise craze? Give it a try and see for yourself.

This little tweak was a game changer for my friend Sami too.

MAKE A DREADED TASK FUN

Think about those mundane tasks that seem to drag on—like folding laundry, mopping the floors, or exercising. Instead of just powering through, why not make them more enjoyable? This simple habit pairing won't necessarily shorten the time, but it can help you reclaim some minutes for happiness. You can focus on the fun part and make the task feel less like a chore.

Some ideas for you to try:

- If you dread doing laundry, turn on your favorite TV show while you fold.
- If you dread sweeping or mopping the floors, try doing it while listening to an audiobook or podcast.
- If you dread exercising, try working out while talking to a friend, or even better, try working out *with* a friend.

When I asked her which chore she dreaded the most because it took the longest, she immediately said, "Laundry!" I asked her, "How long do you think it takes?" She replied, "Forever." I suggested, "Time yourself. You might be surprised."

Later that night, she texted me: "Under ten minutes." Try timing yourself doing a chore you hate and think takes forever. I bet you'll be surprised too.

SET A TIMER FOR YOUR TASK

Remember how setting a timer can make decluttering feel less daunting? The same trick works for any task you dread. By racing against the clock, you'll be amazed at how quickly you can get things done. This simple tweak shows that tasks often take less time than we expect and adds a bit of motivation to help you make the most of your minutes. Give it a try. Set a timer, race the clock, and watch how efficiently you tackle those tasks, reclaiming more minutes for happiness.

Tiny Tweak: Reclaim Hidden Minutes

I finished sending the last email of my workday and noticed I had ten minutes before I needed to pick up my kids from school. I was tempted to grab my phone and scroll through social media. After all, ten minutes doesn't seem like enough time to get anything substantial done, right? We all have those hidden minutes in our day—the ones that come between tasks and feel too short to be helpful.

What if we could make the most of those minutes to accomplish meaningful tasks or, even better, engage in activities that bring us joy and fulfillment? Brigid Schulte called these moments "time confetti."[8] Just like a burst of confetti brings joy and color to a celebration, these hidden minutes can be a delightful treasure in our day. By uncovering and using these hidden minutes with intention, we can add a bit more happiness and efficiency to our lives.

FIND HIDDEN MINUTES

We all have hidden minutes—those little pockets of time that often go unnoticed. Start looking for them like buried treasures and use them intentionally. They add up. They can be used for happiness and joy or for items on your to-do list. It's up to you to decide how to use those moments, but it's incredible how much more valuable they become when we realize they're worth . . . well, our time.

For example, SPL community member Kate timed how long it took to walk the "neighborhood loop." She discovered that it took six minutes. With that information, she'd slip on her shoes and head out the door when she found a few hidden minutes in her day. Within a week, Kate had nearly doubled her daily step count. Cue the confetti. She found buried treasure in her day!

MASTERING **TIME** WITH **GRACE**

Sitting on the couch after my kids had gone to school, I glanced at that first-day-of-school photo and was struck by a deep sense of gratitude. Being their mom has been such a profound gift. I realize now that while I was caught up in the day-to-day, thinking their departure into the world was far off, I wasn't always as intentional with my time as I could have been. I made my share of mistakes and let moments slip by, waiting for more time, and in doing so, I missed out on moments of happiness. But I've learned a lot as I've navigated through those moments. It's not just my kids who have grown and changed—I've grown up too. Reflecting on these years, I see how much I've matured alongside them, discovering that my motherhood journey has helped me be more intentional with the moments and the minutes, no matter how many or few I have in a season.

Perfection isn't the goal in this tweaked, happy life. Instead, it's about learning from our missteps and understanding that failure is not final—it's a great teacher. Just as the sting of a missed opportunity on the ski slopes became the catalyst for facing my fears head-on, missteps with time can guide us toward greater intentionality.

It's not just about squeezing joy into the cracks of our busy days; it's about making joy a nonnegotiable priority. You've identified the activities that bring you the most happiness. Now it's time to plan for them with the same importance as your work tasks or errands. Remember, it's okay if every minute isn't perfectly optimized. The aim is to balance productivity and joy without adding unnecessary pressure.

The true measure of success isn't just in achieving more but in using your time for what truly matters. When the day doesn't go according to plan, tweak your approach with the knowledge that time is not your adversary but a tool you can wield. You're closer to happiness than you think.

USE YOUR TIME

INTENTIONALLY

AND PRIORITIZE

WHAT BRINGS YOU JOY.

10 TEENY-TINY TIME-TRIMMING TWEAKS

1. **Batch cook.** When you cook a meal, double the recipe and freeze half for quick, easy dinners later. It's not much extra work yet double the reward.
2. **Use premade ingredients.** Opt for premade or semi-prepared ingredients to reduce cooking time.
3. **Set time limits.** Allocate specific time blocks for tasks and stick to them to avoid overworking.
4. **Unsubscribe from unnecessary emails.** Reduce inbox clutter by unsubscribing from unwanted newsletters and notifications.
5. **Keep essentials accessible.** Store frequently used items in easy-to-reach places to minimize search time.
6. **Limit email checking.** Designate specific times for checking and responding to emails.
7. **Keep a "to buy" list.** Maintain a list of items you need to buy, to avoid unnecessary shopping trips.
8. **Optimize errand runs.** Combine multiple errands into one trip to save time.
9. **Presort mail.** Quickly sort and handle mail, and recycle and shred what you don't need as soon as it arrives, to avoid piles of paperwork.
10. **Adopt a "do it now" attitude.** If it takes under two minutes, do it now to avoid a backlog.

Part 3
Maximize the Moments

8

PLAN FOR WHAT MATTERS

We were running late for school, but I didn't want to miss my morning walk. Before leaving the house, I threw on an old puffy coat over my pajamas (no bra) and a hat to hide my bedhead. After dropping off the kids, I parked at our local library, popped in my earbuds, and headed out on my morning walk. Did I mention I was wearing ankle weights that could easily be mistaken for a parole tracking device? I was proud of myself for overcoming the excuses—until I walked past the school. My stomach flipped as I noticed a swarm of parents heading inside. In cute clothes, hair done, makeup applied, and, gosh darn it, most likely with appropriate undergarments on. I stood there frozen, racking my brain, flipping through the mind Rolodex wondering what I had forgotten.

It hit me. It was Quincy's kindergarten "Super Reader Day." The day when kids show off to their parents how they can officially read a book. It was a *big* deal. How had I forgotten? My heart sank as

I realized my oversight. I'd failed to put it on the calendar when the note came home. So I jogged back to the car, woefully underdressed, and unstrapped my ankle weights. I didn't want to give anyone a reason to talk as I marched into the school braless, but I was determined not to miss out on this moment with Quincy.

He proudly read to me with a big smile, oblivious to how underdressed I'd arrived compared to the other parents. While it's a funny story now, I'd show up for my kid like that any day. The feeling of being caught off guard was dreadful. I hated the sense of reacting rather than being prepared. So much so that a few months later, those same feelings surged and my heart rate accelerated as I walked by the school again and saw cars parked. More smartly dressed people walked inside. Darn it, not again. I racked my brain to figure out what I'd forgotten, but thankfully, this time, it was nothing for me.

Planning is important. It not only ensures you're appropriately dressed but also helps minimize stress and overwhelm (which I had plenty of on Super Reader Day) and allows you to anticipate what's coming. Good intentions alone don't make things happen; having a good plan does. I've realized that my brain can't be trusted to remember everything on its own. When we take the time to plan, we can ensure that we're doing what needs to be done, as well as what we want, and that we're heading in the right direction. A thoughtful plan makes sure that both the necessities and the joy-giving moments are prioritized.

Good intentions alone don't make things happen; having a good plan does.

NAVIGATING **LIFE** WITH A **PLAN**

Did I mention I was a child of the 1980s? In the olden days, we'd pull out our oversized AAA atlas before any big trip. It came free with my parents' membership. The edges were worn and curled from years of use, and each page showed a maze of highways and cities. Mom would grab her trusty yellow highlighter and carefully map our route. Sometimes we'd even plan for detours to see quirky roadside attractions. Then we'd pile into our wood-paneled station wagon, my sister and me in the backward-facing jump seat, armed with Twizzlers, pumping our arms at truckers in hope of a honk.

Having a plan didn't mean we couldn't stop for ice cream or take a scenic detour—it just gave us the confidence to know where we were headed and how we could adjust if needed. The plan was our guide.

My friend Annē shared a similar realization about life. "I'm not a natural planner," she told me, "but without a plan, I was constantly flying by the seat of my pants, reacting to everything, and missing out on moments that mattered." Like a road trip without a map, life without a plan can leave you frazzled and stressed, always scrambling to catch up.

Like a road trip without a map, life without a plan can leave you frazzled and stressed, always scrambling to catch up.

And that's the thing—planning reduces the mental load. When you don't have a plan, you're more likely to find yourself in situations like, say, showing up to your kid's school braless because you forgot about an important event. Research shows that writing down even a simple plan frees up mental space, letting you focus on the things that matter instead of constantly juggling tasks in your head. According to Cal Newport—a Georgetown computer science professor and focus guru—people who plan their week in advance are more productive and experience less stress.[1]

Having a plan doesn't lock you in—it gives you a road map. A jumping-off point that gives you the flexibility to make tweaks along the way. You can leave room for spontaneous joy like fun road-trip stops at the Corn Palace for a pop-your-own corncob (yes, I got one of those).

With a plan in place, you're ready for opportunities without second-guessing. When a friend texts about a last-minute yoga class, you can confidently say yes or no, knowing exactly what's on your schedule. If an unexpected evening meeting pops up, you can look at your plan and respond with certainty. Just as a road-trip plan helps you enjoy the journey, a plan helps you make the most of your time.

TWEAK BY **PLANNING** YOUR **WEEK**

When it comes to making plans for your life, we're starting with the tiniest tweak that will give you a big bang for your buck: planning your week. It takes less than thirty minutes (that's under 1 percent of your week!) to jot down what you've got going on. And here's the fun part: You can do this any way that works for you. Some might love color-coding (family in red, work in purple, etc.), others prefer a trusty paper planner (I even created the SPL Weekly Plan notepad for this very reason), and some go digital all the way. I even created the SPL Weekly Plan notepad for this very reason. But if you've already got a system that's working, don't mess with it. If you don't, we're going to keep it simple on purpose.

Step 1: Pick a Time to Do This

I like to plan for the next week every Friday. That way, I head into the weekend feeling relaxed, knowing that next week is handled. My mind can fully check out. I even make an accompanying meal plan and grocery list while I'm at it. But there's no magic day for this. Just pick one and mark it on your calendar (see what I did there?). Make this planning time nonnegotiable. Treat it like an important meeting, because it is. It's your strategy session for life, not just work.

Step 2: Jot Down Your Weekly Plan

Grab your planner, a notepad, or even a scrap of paper. (And resist the urge to splurge on a shiny new planner. Remember, the power is in the process, not the product.) Make it fun. If you've got a favorite pen, like my beloved Paper Mate Flair felt-tip pen, use it! While this task might seem boring or just necessary, try pairing it with something you enjoy, like we talked about in the last chapter. Add some fun music, pour yourself a warm cup of tea, or snuggle up with a cozy blanket. This is a tiny hug for your future self!

Write down everything that's happening this week: activities, meetings, appointments, you name it. And don't forget about the hidden to-dos that come with each activity. For example, when my daughter has dance class on Tuesdays, that means I pick her up

PLANNING IS A HUG FOR YOUR FUTURE SELF—A SIMPLE ACT THAT CREATES SPACE FOR CALM, JOY, AND WHAT MATTERS MOST.

from school instead of her riding the bus. It also means I need to make sure I remember to put her dance bag in the car and grab a snack for her, plus an extra water bottle for pickup. These little details become way clearer when you write them down. Add them to your plan to save yourself from last-minute scrambles. You can even set an alarm like we discussed in chapter 6, so you don't forget things like pickups or bags!

Step 3: Put the Plan Where You Can See It

Now that you've got your week mapped out, post it somewhere visible. Trust me, visual reminders are a game changer—they take the pressure off your brain trying to remember it all. When you can see the plan, it's like having a road map in front of you, guiding you through the day and week ahead. I keep ours on the fridge because my family likes to eat, and they'll definitely see it there. Bonus: If you're constantly answering questions like, "What time's practice, Mom?" or "Who's picking me up?" this cuts down on the chaos. Everyone can see the plan.

Step 4: Communicate, Communicate, Communicate

Once the plan is up, make sure everyone is on the same page. My husband and I take a "date" walk on Sunday afternoons and talk through the week—what we call our "meeting of the minds." Then, each night before bed, we quickly check the plan for the next day and make sure we're in sync on pickups, drop-offs, and appointments. It might sound like overkill, but trust me, we've learned the hard way: It's always better to overcommunicate.

Now that you've got your weekly plan in place, you've tackled the first tiny tweak. Remember, the goal isn't perfection, it's progress.

By carving out just a few minutes each week, you're reducing your mental load and giving yourself a clear path forward. And hey, don't worry if things change—you've got the plan as your guide. It's not a rigid schedule.

Life happens. Kids get sick, your car breaks down, or a college friend unexpectedly pops into town. But when you have a plan, you can roll with surprises more easily. It's not about sticking to the plan no matter what; it's about having something to refer to. You can make more informed decisions when (not if) the unexpected strikes. You'll know what can be shifted, what's a priority, and how to rearrange your time without feeling overwhelmed.

When you have a plan, you can roll with surprises more easily.

Now, let's ensure the weekly plan is working for you in this season. We're going to tweak it further to help you navigate your week with even more intention and ease.

ASSESS YOUR WEEKLY PLAN

Amid the COVID-19 pandemic, when everything was shut down, our plates emptied overnight. No activities. No meetings. No trips. No visitors. When things started to come back online, I realized how busy we had been. I posted a picture of myself holding a plate and wrote this post on Instagram:

> Why am I holding a plate? For the first time, maybe ever, our plate has literally been emptied of nearly every nonessential

> extracurricular activity. . . . Our plate has been cleared, and as a result, we have a tremendous gift, an opportunity moving forward, should we choose to take it.
>
> We can carefully choose what goes back on our plate. . . . It might not look like it did before, maybe it will look exactly the same, but before you fill it up, know full well WHY it's something worthy of valuable space on your plate. . . .
>
> New sign-ups for fall are starting to hit our inboxes. Listen closely to your heart. To your children's hearts. What have you missed? What are you not missing at all? Fill your plate with purpose. Don't forget to leave margin for dessert, the good stuff of life.

While I never wish to return to that time, I still remember how I assessed every activity and whether it really belonged in our schedule. Sometimes things are on your schedule because you said yes to them in another season. It was worthwhile then, but maybe the season has changed. It's good to regularly assess what we spend our time on and ensure it's what matters most. And leave space for dessert.

I was part of a women's group called Philanthropic Educational Organization (P.E.O.) for years. When I was a young stay-at-home mom, it was my social outlet. I served as president and was heavily involved, but as my kids aged, I felt the pull to be home with them. Even if there wasn't anything on the calendar, I wanted that time to enjoy family dinner. It was really hard for me to say no to my women's group, but I realized a no in that season was a yes to what really mattered right then—and it wasn't a no forever.

Look at your calendar and assess if there are activities or events taking up valuable space in your week that you can declutter. Just like with physical clutter, requests, obligations, club meetings, and one-off events are always sneaking onto our schedules. Check in to be sure they are still what matters most to you. A good thing like that P.E.O. group might have been right in a different season, and it's okay if it isn't any longer.

IT'S OKAY TO **SAY NO**

Saying no can be tough. We often feel obligated to say yes to every invitation, request, or opportunity that comes our way, fearing we'll disappoint others or miss out on something important. Take a moment to reflect: Have you said yes to something out of guilt or obligation recently?

When saying no or yes to a future obligation, a tiny tweak is to say, "Let me check my calendar." This is a good habit, even if you think you might say yes, as it ensures you have the space and time to think through what that yes or no would mean for your schedule. Every yes is a no to something else. As Steve Jobs put it, "It's only by saying no that you can concentrate on the things that are really important."[2]

> **Your plate doesn't have to be overflowing to say no. Sometimes white space is exactly what our schedules need.**

If you decide to decline an offer after consideration, you can simply say, "It doesn't fit in my schedule." I once heard someone say, "My plate is as full as I like." I loved that, because your plate doesn't have to be overflowing to say no. Sometimes white space is exactly what your schedule needs.

CAN YOU **DELEGATE** OR **OUTSOURCE**?

Simple Purposeful Living transitioned from a side hustle to a full-time job a few years ago. The shift happened gradually, and I tried to keep up with everything I had always done, but I quickly fell behind. I had a decision to make. After weighing the pros and cons, Scott and I hired a monthly cleaning service. While I love keeping things tidy, none of us were particularly great at deep cleaning (don't look at my kids' toilets right before the cleaning crew comes!).

At first, I struggled and felt ashamed, like I had failed by not doing everything myself. But then I realized something important: Not everything I'm juggling is made of glass. As Nora Roberts wisely said, "The key to juggling is to know that some of the balls you have in the air are made of plastic and some are made of glass."[3] Cleaning the house? That's a plastic ball. Time with my family? That's glass—if I let it fall, it could shatter.

When we delegate, we're not just unloading tasks—we're creating opportunities for others to step in.

Whether at work or home, there are tasks we do because we've always done them, but that could be handled by someone else. It's hard to let go because we often think, *I can do it better myself*, or *It'll take longer to explain than to just do it*. But when we delegate, we're not

TINY TWEAKS FOR PLANNING

TINY TWEAK: PRACTICE WHITE SPACE

I remember the first time I visited the Louvre Museum, I couldn't wait to see the *Mona Lisa*. Turns out she's much smaller than I expected. I went all the way to Paris for that (still worth it, but seriously, she's tiny!). What really struck me was how the entire wall around her is left blank, giving her the space to truly stand out.

That's exactly how I want you to think about white space in your life. Just as the *Mona Lisa* needs room to shine, your Happiness Spaces need room to breathe. Without intentional white space, even the things that bring us the most joy can feel crowded and overshadowed by the endless rush of life.

When you're planning your week, don't just focus on squeezing in all your tasks. Make sure you're carving out that white space too. Look at your schedule. Do you have enough time for your Happiness Spaces? Space for your soul to breathe? Opportunities to take the scenic route, say yes to impromptu ice cream, or enjoy yoga with a friend? If not, this is your chance to create it. Where can you be fiercely protective of your time, so you can create and protect those Happiness Spaces?

Just because your calendar is open doesn't mean you have to fill it. Protect your time like the rare gem it is.

TINY TWEAK: PUT IT ON THE CALENDAR

If good intentions don't make things happen and a plan does, we need to get in the regular habit of putting what matters on the calendar. A few years ago, I wanted to host our annual reindeer games party. It's a highly competitive series of games that include musical chairs and winding up reindeer to see whose goes the farthest. I texted out the date in November because I had learned the hard way the previous year that if you don't put what you want on the calendar for the holiday season, it won't happen. (My parents taught me this well. My cousin's boyfriend even laughed when he found out my parents were planning Thanksgiving, not for this year, but for the next year. But they knew that if they didn't schedule it early, getting us all there would never happen.)

Putting things on the calendar goes for major events and everyday things. Scott and I share a long-range calendar that syncs with his work and mine for events that affect each other or our family. If something comes up that involves both of us—like a dinner, work travel, or a kid's game—we put it on the calendar and invite each other to that event. It helps us plan logistics, like who's picking up whom and what time dinner will be.

Here's where the breakdown happened for me with Quincy's Super Reader Day: I didn't put it on the calendar when he brought home the note in his take-home folder. And while oversights happen because we are all human, they're fewer when we make the effort to put important events on the calendar as soon as they come up.

TINY TWEAK: PLAN STANDING DATES

In addition to one-off events, standing dates are a great way to ensure you regularly connect with those who matter most. A few summers ago, my friend Teri set up a standing coffee chat with our friend group every Thursday at 7 a.m. It wasn't a fancy brunch or dinner, but it worked—and we stayed connected all summer long without having to constantly coordinate. It was simple, effective, and meaningful.

Scott and I have a standing date on Fridays for lunch, since we both work from home on that day. Sometimes we go out; sometimes we eat on the back deck. The point is, it's a time we've set aside to intentionally connect. Standing dates make it easier to nurture relationships without feeling like you're scrambling to find time.

Do you have standing dates with friends, your spouse, or even yourself? If not, now's a great time to set them up. It could be as simple as a walk with a friend, a coffee meetup, or even a workout class together. The goal of a standing date is to make it easier to connect with those you care about.

just unloading tasks—we're creating opportunities for others to step in, whether it's learning a new skill, taking on responsibility, or simply helping out.

Another plastic ball I passed off was folding laundry. The kids fold and put away their own clothes now. At first, I felt guilty, but sometimes we need to look at all the perspectives. It lightened my load, and since we're raising future adults, they're getting the chance to practice valuable life skills. And if the drawers aren't perfect, it's just a plastic ball—it won't break!

Consider what tasks you can delegate, whether it's a colleague who can take on a project at work or a family member who can help with household chores. If you have the means, think about outsourcing tasks that are eating up your time, like cleaning, grocery shopping, or meal prep. Services like these can free up precious hours in your week, allowing you to focus on what truly matters.

I'm still learning to say no and delegate as well. With each practice, my no muscle and my delegation muscle get stronger. It becomes easier to let go of commitments that no longer serve me. Everyone's needs and stamina are different, and that's okay. You don't have to carry every ball—especially the plastic ones!

AVOID THE **ANT TRAP** OF BUSYNESS

Henry David Thoreau once said, "It is not enough to be industrious; so are the ants. The question is: What are we industrious about?"[4] Friend, let's take a moment to consider this. We often scurry around like ants, filling our days with endless tasks and appointments because we've been told that being busy equals success. We wear our busyness like a badge of honor. But here's the truth: Being busy doesn't automatically mean we're being productive or successful. We might just be making ourselves exhausted.

True productivity isn't about how packed your calendar is. It's about striking a balance between the necessary tasks that keep our lives running smoothly and the nourishing activities that feed our souls. It's about being intentional with our time, making space for both work and play, for both responsibility and rest.

I remember one time feeling weird about sharing on social media that I took a nap. I worried it would make me seem unmotivated, like I couldn't hack it, especially when it feels like the rest of the world is constantly hustling. Even when I needed time offline, I felt guilty, like I should be able to keep going without taking a break. But here's the thing: In the United States, most people don't even take the time off they've earned. In fact, many workers leave their paid vacation days unused every year to appear more dedicated or productive.

Just as we leave a cushion in our monthly budgets for miscellaneous expenses, we need to leave space in our calendars for rest and spontaneous fun.

But for what? Sacrificing rest doesn't make us better at our jobs or more successful. It leads to burnout, stress, and exhaustion. Arianna Huffington, cofounder of *The Huffington Post*, learned this the hard way. After years of relentless striving, Arianna collapsed from exhaustion in 2007. She realized that no amount of success was worth sacrificing her health, happiness, and relationships. From that moment, she became a powerful advocate for redefining success—not as busyness or wealth but as a life that includes well-being, balance, and rest.[5]

This is where planning comes in. Just as we leave a cushion in our monthly budgets for miscellaneous expenses, we need to leave space in our calendars for rest and spontaneous fun. Life happens: an unexpected opportunity to spend time with a friend, a beautiful day that calls for a walk, or simply a moment to take a nap. Without that buffer of white space—those Happiness Spaces—we risk filling every moment with tasks, leaving no room for joy or recharging.

How do you know if you're just being busy like an ant or if you're truly being purposeful? Take a moment to look at your calendar and reflect on these questions:

- Is every hour of your day filled with activities or tasks?
- Can you find any white space in your calendar for rest and spontaneity?
- Do you often feel exhausted and never fully recharged?
- Are activities that nourish your mind, body, and soul consistently pushed aside for "more important" tasks?
- Do you find yourself agreeing to commitments out of obligation rather than genuine interest or necessity?

If you answered yes to most of these questions, you might be caught in the "ant trap" of busyness. But don't worry! Recognizing this is the first step toward change.

THE WHAT MATTERS LIST VS. THE **BUCKET LIST**

I used to be a bucket-list junkie, writing out all the things I wanted to do each season. But I found that I'd often feel discouraged at the end of the season when only half of the list was completed. I shifted my approach to something simpler: a What Matters list. Now I ask my kids to name one thing they really want to do during that season or holiday, and I put it on the calendar. Last year, at Christmas, they asked to decorate gingerbread houses, shop for their siblings' gift exchange, and do our boys vs. girls ornament challenge. We didn't go on the Polar Express, participate in every local holiday event, or bake dozens of cookies for our neighbors. Instead of aiming for fifty things, we focused on a few that mattered most. This tweak has brought more joy and eliminated the pressure of trying to do it all.

PLAN TO **STAY PRESENT**

I used to always be thinking about what was next, never being fully present in the moment. I'd be at the apple orchard but my mind would be someplace else. I hated it. But over time and with practice, I learned to trust that my planning would guide me, allowing me to be more fully present. Now, whether I'm sitting around the table with my kids, enjoying the beach, or loading up my basket with the Jonagold apples that Quincy plucks from the branches, I can relax knowing that my plan has things taken care of.

That's where we want to get to with planning. A plan is not meant to be a cage that keeps you locked in future thinking; it's a safety net that supports you. A well-thought-out plan creates a

TWEAKS TO STAY PRESENT

1. **Trust the plan.** Once you've made your plan, trust it. Give yourself permission to be present, knowing that you've already set a course for what's coming next.
2. **Practice mindful moments.** My therapist taught me the 5-4-3-2-1 method and I practice it every morning. Since I practice it regularly, when I find myself not in the moment, I can use it to bring me back.

   5: Notice five things you can see around you.
   4: Focus on four things you can feel.
   3: Listen for three sounds.
   2: Take in two scents.
   1: Focus on one thing you can taste.

   This simple exercise helps ground you in the moment and keeps your mind from drifting too far into the future.
3. **Lean in to your white space and schedule Happiness Spaces.** Remember the "white space" we created earlier in the chapter? Use those moments intentionally, not just for productivity or catching up, but also for breathing, being present, and savoring the life happening right in front of you.

   White space is where you can slow down and recharge. To make the most of it, plan for moments of stillness and joy—whether it's a walk, time with loved ones, or simply sitting with a good book. By scheduling this downtime, you create room to enjoy life now while staying organized for the future. This balance allows you to live fully in the present while trusting that your plan will take care of what's next.
4. **Revisit and revise.** If your plan starts feeling like a burden instead of a support, don't be afraid to adjust. A flexible plan is key to feeling both prepared for the future and present in the now.

foundation, giving you the freedom to live more fully in the moment without worrying about what's next. When done right, planning helps you show up for the present with peace of mind.

But if you find that your plans *are* pulling you out of the moment, I've included some tiny tweaks to stay present on the next page—practical tweaks to help you right the sails.

A plan is not meant to be a cage that keeps you locked in future thinking; it's a safety net that supports you.

Ultimately, the goal of planning isn't about fixating on what's next; it's about creating a structure that allows you to fully enjoy the present. With your plan in place, you've given yourself the freedom to be here, now, and enjoy the white space and moments that matter.

PLANNING CREATES THE PATHWAY TO HAPPINESS

I exited my car with the canvas bag tucked over my shoulder. A picnic blanket and Subway sandwiches were inside, per Lucille's request. I was dressed in a cute new sweater. My hair was brushed. My heart beat excitedly, not out of anxiety but out of anticipation of spending time with my girl as she read the poetry she had prepared for the Mother's Day poetry picnic. After my debacle at Quincy's Super Reader Day a few months before, I'd developed the habit of planning, so when she excitedly handed me the note detailing the event, I grabbed my phone and put it on the calendar. Then, when I made my weekly plan, I noted it. I would be ready. There were no feelings of stress or anxiety. The plan helped me to show up on purpose, helped me to be fully present with my girl, and created space for happiness and what mattered most.

Life will happen whether we make a plan or not, but we can tweak our lives to be proactive instead of reactive. When we plan intentionally—whether it's white space, standing dates, or special events—we simplify life and create space for what truly matters. Taking a few minutes to jot down a weekly plan is a tool to help you stay ahead of the chaos and ensure you're not just checking off tasks but living a life that aligns with your values. Look at it and be sure that what matters is represented. Now grab your pom-poms and cheer with me: "Keep life on track! Planning's power has your back!"

> **We can tweak our lives to be proactive instead of reactive.**

5 P'S OF MEAL PLANNING

Feeding your family can be stressful. But making the tweak to have a simple plan not only reduces decision fatigue and overwhelm but also streamlines your life. When you know what's for dinner, you eliminate the daily scramble of figuring out what to cook. This clarity allows you to prioritize gathering around the table and connecting with your family. Those shared meals are where we bond, exchange stories, and create lasting memories. Your future self will be giving you a big ole hug for taking a few minutes to plan!

1. **Plan.** Plan your week. Grab your weekly meal planner (I've got a great one in my shop if you need one!). If your evenings are packed with activities like mine are, plan meals that work with your schedule.
2. **Pick.** Choose meals your family likes and that fit your schedule. Stuck on ideas? Try a weekly rotation. For example, Meatless Mondays, Taco Tuesdays, Slow Cooker Wednesdays. This reduces decision fatigue big-time!
3. **Prep.** Make your grocery list. Include everything you need for dinners, plus breakfast, lunch, snacks, and staples. **Pro tip:** Keep your grocery list on the counter. Everyone can add to the list throughout the week.

4. **Purchase.** Hit the store with your list. One of the many reasons I love meal planning is that I shop only once a week. Talk about saving time and money!
5. **Peace.** Enjoy the peace of mind that comes with a stress-free week. No more "What's for dinner?" panic!

HERE'S A SAMPLE MEAL ROTATION TO GET YOU STARTED:

Monday: Pasta night
Tuesday: Taco night
Wednesday: Slow cooker meals
Thursday: Sandwiches or wraps
Friday: Pizza night
Saturday: Grilled meats with sides
Sunday: Leftovers (or as Scott's grandmother called them, "planned-overs"!)

Remember, the best meal plan is one that works for your family. It's not about being perfect; it's about making life easier. Keep a few backup meals on hand for when things go sideways (because they will!). I always have some mac and cheese boxes and PB&J fixings ready to go. You can also download a free weekly menu rotation printable at https://simplepurposefulliving.com/meal-rotation/.

9

AUTOMATE WHAT MATTERS

While parked in the high school parking lot, I sent a GIF of a woman pulling her hair out to my friend-group chat. *Yep, that's me*, I thought, running my fingers through my bedhead-tangled locks. Summer had barely begun, and I already felt like I was drowning in a sea of high school sports schedules, kids' social lives, and the never-ending household chores. And, oh, work—let's not forget about that.

As I stared at the mess of our weekly plan on my phone, my eyes started to cross. How was I supposed to get my high schooler to football practice when my middle schooler needed to be across town for dance? My phone pinged—a text from my assistant, Keri. "Are we still on for our meeting today?" My eyes widened. I'd completely forgotten. "Shoot, I need to get it together," I muttered, scrambling to confirm the meeting.

The day felt like one chaotic blur. I was running from one task to the next, feeling the weight pressing down on my shoulders. And, of course, the laundry was piling up, we were all running low on undies (apparently, it's frowned upon to turn them inside out), and the chicken meant for dinner was still rock-solid in the freezer.

By the end of the day, I was disgruntled, sweaty, and stinky—desperately needing a shower. *Why does it feel like my life is spinning out of control?* I wondered. After all, I'd made a plan. My mind raced with all the tasks and responsibilities screaming for my attention. I hated feeling this way. I did what I'd learned to do: I asked myself, *What tweak can make this easier?*

I realized I felt so off-balance because when summer blew in, my routine went out the window. I missed its structure. It felt like day eight of Christmas vacation. You know, when you're full of cream-cheese dips, still wearing stretchy pants, and not sure what day it is. You're craving something, a tweak, and that something is structure (aka routine). There was a hitch in our giddyap, but I could update my routine to fit this season and get back to galloping along. At least we would have clean undies and thawed chicken while still being flexible for every day's surprises—because we all know there are always surprises.

Life can get complicated, especially when juggling your demands. Seasons are constantly shifting. Whether it's heading into tax season, deciding to retire, or finding balance during the holidays, there are still things that need to be done (laundry and meals) and things you want to get done so your life feels fulfilling—those things that bring you joy and happiness. Things like coffee with friends, piano lessons, and curling up with a good book. The problem is, when life gets harried, if what matters isn't automated, it might not get done.

If what matters isn't automated, it might not get done.

TWEAK AN UNBALANCED **LIFE** WITH A **GOOD ROUTINE**

This is where routines come in. They both simplify life and ensure what matters gets done. I love a two-for-one deal, don't you?

In the last chapter, we talked about how having a plan gives you a road map to follow, like using my family's old AAA atlas. But just as GPS made travel more manageable with turn-by-turn navigation, routines make our plans easier by providing step-by-step directions. They make our plans actionable, helping us move through tasks with less stress, and in the correct order, getting us to where we want to go with ease.

In James Clear's wildly popular book, *Atomic Habits*, he talked about how goals or plans are about the results you want to achieve (the destination). He said we spend a lot of time thinking about the destination. *School starts at 8:00 a.m. Lucille has dance class on Tuesdays at 5:00 p.m. The kids need to go to bed at 8:00 p.m.* We spend little time thinking about how we'll successfully make that happen. *How can I get out of the house on time? What needs to be done? How will Lucille get to dance on Tuesdays? What needs to happen for the kids to be in bed by 8:00 p.m.?* Clear said the critical component of arriving at your goal or destination is thinking through the systems and processes (the routines) that lead to those results. He said, "You do not rise to the level of your goals. You fall to the level of your systems."[1]

If you've ever felt like I did that crazy summer morning, it might be because your systems and routines are not optimized, but the good news is—you guessed it—it doesn't take an overhaul. It takes a tweak here and there to set up your routines so you can get out of the house, pick up the kids, and put the kids to bed with less stress. Sound amazing? You can do it!

LITTLE **TWEAKS** FOR **BIG RESULTS**

That morning as I sat in the high school parking lot wondering what had happened to my life, I asked myself, *What tweak can I make to our routine to make it simpler and less stressful?* I resisted overhauling our typical weekly routine and aimed for the simplest tweak. We tend to overcomplicate when it's not necessary. Rather than throwing it all out, I got curious, paused, stepped back, and determined what had to be done. What simple tweak could I make?

I knew immediately. The night before, I needed to do a quick check of our weekly schedule on the fridge. I'd already mapped out our week, so I knew what had to be done (remember that from the last chapter?). I just needed to create a system for us to get it done. We'd have a quick family meeting (a fancy term for a logistical conversation) to check the schedule and walk through our day as a family, and ensure everyone would get where they needed to go (who drives whom there and back?). A simple tweak, and we had a routine, a system. With any luck, I'd stop pulling out my hair.

Notice it wasn't a multistep process and didn't take lots of time. Routines can be simple. In fact, simple, small routines are easier to maintain. I used to forget to water my plants until I made a little routine. On Sundays, I water my plants while I make lunch. My plants no longer look like they're dying, and I don't have to question when I last watered them. Every evening after dinner, I spend ten minutes tidying up the kitchen. As a result, it's a blank slate ready for tomorrow's adventure. Before I go to sleep, I spend at least fifteen minutes reading a book. I made teeny-tiny tweaks to build a teeny-tiny routine that helps me automate what matters, know what to expect, bring comfort to the chaos, and reduce decision fatigue.

BUILD A SIMPLE ROUTINE

Step 1: Identify a Pain Point

We all have at least one nagging area of our life that just feels clunkier or harder than it should be. Something we know we should be doing but just *don't*. For me, it was washing my face before bed. I used to lazily drag myself from the couch to bed, skipping the face-washing step far too often. Then I turned forty, and wrinkles were showing up on my face like creases in a bedsheet. I realized I needed to make a change.

What's your pain point? Maybe it's something small, like not drinking enough water or being too rushed in the morning. When you know the answer, you can start to automate.

Step 2: Build on What's Already Working

To begin washing my face, I asked myself, *What am I already doing that I can build on?* Since the issue was that I was too tired to wash my face at bedtime, I realized it wasn't the routine itself that didn't work—it was *when* I was doing it. I asked myself, *When am I not tired and still on my feet with the energy to walk to the bathroom and wash my face consistently?* Most nights, I was already up and about cleaning the kitchen after dinner. I figured I could tack on my face-washing routine and put my pajamas on right after that.

By now you know I have no problem leaving the house braless. If I needed to do a carpool later that night, I could just put on a sweatshirt, but my face would be washed. There's no need to reinvent the wheel—just add a tiny tweak to what's already part of your day.

S.J. Scott, in his book *Habit Stacking*, explained the power of building on what's working: "The easiest way to create a new habit is to tie it into a current habit you're already doing consistently."[2] By stacking my face-washing habit onto cleaning the kitchen, I found a way to fit it naturally into my routine without extra effort.

What's something you're already doing that you can build on? Maybe it's prepping lunch for the next day in glass bowls while cleaning up from dinner, or putting away laundry during your evening wind down. Use what's working and give yourself the gift of a routine that fits seamlessly into your day.

Step 3: Make It Obvious

To make sure I stuck with it, I made the routine obvious and easy. I put my face wash, bio-retinol, and lotion right on the bathroom counter. That way it's impossible to miss. I even told my teenage daughter I needed accountability because I knew she'd ask if I'd done it, or she'd outright remind me. (Thank goodness for teens, right?) Having visible or auditory cues can help you stick with the routine. How can you make your new routine obvious? A step-by-step checklist, phone alarm reminder, or sticky note might be just what you need.

Step 4: Go in an Order That Makes Sense

Think about what order makes sense in your day. For me, the right order was heading to the bathroom after cleaning the kitchen while I was still on my feet. No need to add more steps—just a tweak to an already-existing process. My routine didn't work before because I wasn't going in the best order for me.

Here's another example: If your morning routine feels rushed because you're scrambling to pack lunches after breakfast, leaving you frazzled and sending off lunch boxes missing key components, try going in an order that makes more sense—like packing lunches the night before. It saves time and reduces stress in the morning. Going in the right order can make all the difference.

What's the logical order for your new routine? Look at your pain point and place it where it naturally fits. When you follow the right order, your routine will feel like a natural part of your day instead of an extra task you need to remember.

Step 5: Keep It Simple, Sweetheart (KISS)

As you establish or tweak your routine, remember to KISS: Keep it simple, sweetheart! I didn't tackle a long list of bedtime rituals. I just washed my face, applied bio-retinol, applied lotion, brushed my teeth, and put on my pj's. No stretching, no meditation—nothing more. If it's too complicated, it won't happen. Focus on the essentials and make it doable. What's the simplest version of your routine? Keep only the steps that matter most, and don't overcomplicate things.

Greg McKeown, in *Essentialism*, explained, "Essentialism is not about how to get more things done; it's about how to get the *right* things done."[3] Just like we decluttered our house and left white space in our calendar, keeping our routine simple is key. Too many steps or trying to fit in too many things will overwhelm. Instead, focus on what truly needs to be done and let go of the rest.

ROUTINES ARE THE BACKBONE OF A SIMPLER LIFE—STRONG ENOUGH TO HOLD IT ALL, AND FLEXIBLE ENOUGH TO BEND WITH IT.

You can always build on automated and established routines later, but first, ask yourself, *What's the most important thing here?* If your kids' bedtime routine is taking forever and pushing bedtime back, simplify it. Ask yourself, *What matters most?* Maybe it's just putting on pajamas, brushing teeth, going to the bathroom, and reading one book. You can always add more later, but overcomplicated routines are difficult to maintain and automate. Start small and essentialize.

Step 6: Practice, Practice, Practice

Sometimes I forget to wash my face, and you know what? That's okay. We're all human. I have a sticky note on the sink and accountability with my daughter to help me stay on track. Practice makes progress, not perfection. When I was a first-grade teacher, we would practice our classroom procedures over and over again. That repetition over time automated the process—my students knew exactly what to do without thinking. It's the same with routines. As long as it's simple, with practice you will make progress.

In our culture, we often get impatient and expect perfection right away. On average, it takes sixty-six days for a new behavior to become automatic.[4] Some habits take more or less time, but the key is consistency. Think about how long you've been brushing your teeth. I've been brushing mine for as long as I can remember—that's more than fifteen thousand days of practice! It took time to build that habit, and the same will be true for any new routine.

What can you do to practice your new routine? Give yourself grace, remember to keep it simple, involve a friend or family member, and stick with it until it feels like second nature. Success is found just on the other side of consistency.

Step 7: Be Flexible

Routines aren't set in stone—they're rhythms that can shift. If I'm out with friends for dinner, I tweak the routine and wash my face when I get home. Routines should serve you, not stress you out. How can you stay flexible with your routine? Remember, some days you'll do the whole routine, and other days you'll just hit the essentials—and that's perfectly fine.

Think of your routine like the verses of a song. Some days, you'll have time to sing all five verses; other days, you'll only have time for one verse and a chorus. What matters is knowing what's essential. My sister, Ellen, my cousin Madelynne, and I were chatting, and Ellen and I agreed that daily showers are negotiable for us, but that was not the case for my cousin. Showers are essential for her. It's important to know what matters most to you and honor that, but if everything matters equally, it's going to get dicey when you need to cut something.

Life happens—sometimes your water heater breaks, you oversleep, or you forget to thaw the chicken for dinner. Routines are meant to bend and flow with the rhythm of the day. If they don't bend, they'll break. Ask yourself, *What can I let go of when things get tight, and what's nonnegotiable for me?* Understanding this will help you maintain a routine that supports you, not overwhelms you.

ONE **ROUTINE** DOESN'T **FIT ALL**

Wouldn't it be nice if I could hand deliver the perfect routine that would simplify your life and save you from stress? I wish I could.

But the reality is, one routine doesn't fit all—just like one mapped-out route won't get everyone from where they are to their desired destination. You'll want to personalize your routine to fit your lifestyle.

The best routine is the one that aligns with what matters most to you.

Think of it like choosing a route on your Maps app. Some of us prefer the scenic route, while others pick the one with the fewest turns. Maybe you avoid toll roads, while someone else loves their expediency. None of these routes are best—they're just different, just like no single routine is superior. You get to decide what matters to you and build a routine that fits your life right now.

For example, I *must* make my bed every morning—it's non-negotiable. But as I confessed earlier, I can easily skip a morning shower if time is tight, while some of you might cringe at the thought. You might leave the house showered but with an unmade bed. That's why routines are personal. The best routine is the one that aligns with what matters most to you.

THE **ROUTINE ROADBLOCK** YOU DIDN'T SEE COMING

For years, my mornings felt like chaos—rushing out the door with my hair on fire, always running late, no matter how early I'd started. I couldn't understand why things never seemed to go as planned. The truth is, I was falling into the trap of the Planning Fallacy. What is that?

It's when we underestimate how long things take. We think we can do everything faster than we really can, leading to unrealistic expectations and constant stress. That's why we're always surprised when "just getting ready" or running a "quick errand" takes twice as long as expected.

The problem wasn't my routine—and it might not be yours either. I thought I had more time than I really did. So I made a tiny tweak. Instead of changing my routine, I decided to time it. I clocked everything—from waking the kids to making breakfast and getting out the door. Turns out, my "five-minute" morning routine was actually taking fifteen minutes, and getting the kids ready wasn't a twenty-minute task—it took closer to forty. No wonder I was always running late.

With this new information, I made a small but powerful change: I started waking up the kids fifteen minutes earlier. That tiny tweak gave us the extra time we needed and transformed our mornings from frantic to calm.

START WITH THE **DESTINATION** IN MIND

Just like your weekly plan serves as your road map for the week ahead, your routines help you reach your destinations—those goals and priorities that matter most. Knowing your priorities—whether it's fostering deeper connections over dinner, hitting professional milestones, or simply keeping your plants alive—will guide you through the week.

Routines are the systems that make our plans actionable. They are the steps that help you go from point A to point B with ease. Most of us already have some kind of routine for each day of the week, but have we considered why we do things the way we do? Whether it's how you begin your mornings or how you wind down your evenings, this routine can support the goals in your weekly plan. Just like a good road trip starts with a clear route mapped out, a successful week starts with routines that help you navigate your day.

> **Tweak your routines to make them your own. and resist comparing to someone else's. Don't compare—be inspired and create a routine that works for you.**

I'm going to share some keystone routines as inspiration to get you thinking, because it's always helpful to learn from others. But remember, the key is to tweak your routines to make them your own. The casualty here would be comparing your routine to someone else's instead of personalizing it to fit your life. Don't compare—be inspired and create a routine that works for you.

KEYSTONE DAILY ROUTINES

Keystone daily routines are the essential activities that provide the structure for your day, helping everything else fall into place. These routines, like the bones of your body, give strength and stability to your routine, holding everything up. When your routines are in place, they help you move through the day more easily and with less stress.

TWEAKS FOR FINDING EXTRA TIME

If you find yourself constantly rushing or feeling overwhelmed, try these tweaks:

1. **Time your routine.** Pick a daily task that feels rushed and use a timer to see how long it really takes.
2. **Adjust your schedule.** Compare the actual time to what you expected, then adjust your schedule to give yourself a realistic buffer. A small change, like waking up fifteen minutes earlier, can make a huge difference.

Remember, it's not always the routine that needs tweaking—it's understanding how long things really take. Once you do, you'll find it easier to create a routine that works for you.

Morning Routine

My morning routine begins before my kids awaken (because these days I'm sleeping through the night—something I couldn't do when they were little). I get up, go to the bathroom, grab my robe, and brush my hair (because bedhead drives me batty—see, routines are personal). Then I brew myself a cup of Nespresso, usually around 6:00 a.m. I sit in silence, maybe watch the sunrise, read a passage of the Bible and a devotional, pray, and write in my gratitude journal. Afterward, I make sure the kids are up before I wash my face, brush my teeth, put my hair in a ponytail, and put on my workout clothes. I make my bed, and by then the kids—who get themselves dressed—come down for breakfast. They're old enough now to read the lunch menu and decide between hot or cold lunch, making their lunches accordingly. I've become more of a coach on the sidelines, reminding them of their routines as they need it.

Your morning routine might involve different elements, like getting up for a walk, spending quiet time reading, or simply making sure you're showered and dressed before the kids wake up. Or, if you don't have kids, it might be savoring a cup of coffee in peace, journaling, or listening to a podcast before heading to work. Whatever it looks like, the goal is to set a positive tone for the rest of your day.

Evening Routine

My evening routine starts after dinner. Whoever is home clears the table, the kids put their dishes in the dishwasher, and Scott and I tag team cleaning the kitchen. We put leftovers in glass storage containers for our lunches the next day. This simplifies grabbing Scott's lunch in the morning. I do a quick wipe-down of the counters, put away any counter clutter (because, as we've discussed, a little tidying each day keeps the clutter away), and do a quick vacuum. We start the dishwasher (the kids unload it in the morning), and then I get ready for bed.

I wash my face and brush my teeth (which helps cut down on late-night snacking—an unintended win), and then we hang out as a family. We do carpool runs before the alarm goes off for the little kids to prepare for bed. We do a quick family tidy of the main spaces before the little two put on their pajamas, brush their teeth, and read a book (Scott and I take turns reading). Then I usually sneak into bed to read after putting my phone to sleep. Scott and I chat about our day and what's on tap for the next day, and the big kids often come in to say good night and chat too. Lights are out around 9:30 or 10:00 p.m.

Your evening routine might involve tidying up, setting out clothes for the next day, or winding down with a book. It will likely look different from mine—and that's the point! This routine works for me right now, but it will shift as my kids move into new phases of life, just like yours will evolve over time. The goal is to create a routine that works for now—one that serves your current season, knowing it can be adjusted as life changes. I'm not into TV at all (my family thinks I'm weird for that), but maybe watching your favorite show is a key part of how you wind down. The goal is to find what works for you and creates a smooth, stress-free transition from day to night. This is your chance to prepare for tomorrow, practice some self-care, make the next day easier, and allow yourself to relax before bed.

Mealtimes

It doesn't matter how busy the day is, my family always expects to eat. *The audacity, am I right?* Having some structure around mealtimes helps simplify the process and foster connection. I find that food brings the kids to the table, but connection keeps us there. That's why putting a little effort into a plan and routine around mealtimes is important to me. But even if you live alone or don't have a family to feed, meal planning simplifies life by providing nourishment and a way to care for yourself—and it's also an easy way to host friends and enjoy dinner together.

In the last chapter's resource, I shared how I meal plan weekly.

This weekly routine (more on that in a minute) sets us up for success on the daily. For breakfast and lunch, we keep it simple. Have you ever been to the Cheesecake Factory? I love that restaurant, but their menu is like a novel, with twenty-plus pages of entrée options. If they simplified the menu, the wait time would go down drastically—it's just too much. On the flip side, when you go to a restaurant with just three to four options, it's easy to decide what to have. We adopted that mindset for breakfast and lunch.

Breakfast might be bagels with cream cheese, Greek yogurt parfaits, frozen waffles, or eggs. The kids can choose one—*boom*, done! Same with lunch. Keeping it simple means less decision fatigue and smoother mornings. Then, dinner is planned out in advance, and we sit down with whoever is home. Consistent mealtimes create a natural rhythm for the day and help us connect as a family.

When you make your plan for the week, it's important to consider *when* you're going to eat dinner each day. This helps determine what kind of meal will work best. Busy workday? Maybe it's a slow cooker meal or something you can prep ahead of time. When my kids were little, we ate at 5:30 p.m. every day, and if Scott wasn't walking in the door, I was texting him because the kids were hungry and, well, put a fork in me, I was done!

Now we eat when it makes the most sense in our weekly plan (which is why planning is key), but the routine remains the same every night. I line up the food on the counter and ring the dinner bell—yes, just like Pavlov's dog. The kids go through the meal line, usually youngest to oldest, and then we sit down and pray with whoever is home. After dinner, the kids ask to be excused, and everyone helps clear the table and clean up. This structure helps everyone know what to expect and lightens my load. It also brings calm to the chaos and encourages independence.

A small tweak to allow more time might be all it takes to shift from stress to calm.

These routines—whether it's how we start our mornings, wind down in the evenings, or gather for meals—are like the keystone in a building. They hold everything else together, providing structure and stability for each day. When these routines are in place, life feels smoother and there's more space for connection, rest, and joy.

Think through your daily routines. Is there a time or task that feels harder than it should? Are you squeezing too much into a space that can't hold it all, leaving you feeling overwhelmed? Remember the "roadblock" we talked about earlier. It might not be your routine that's the issue but the time you've allotted for it. Take an opportunity to time yourself and see if your expectations match the actual time needed. A small tweak to allow more time might be all it takes to shift from stress to calm.

Routines don't have to be complicated, but they do need to work for you. A small tweak can make all the difference, simplifying your life and making room for what matters most. Look at your daily routines. What's one small change you can make to bring more ease and flow to your day?

KEYSTONE WEEKLY ROUTINES

Most people focus on daily routines, but to make those really work, keystone weekly routines are a game changer. If daily routines are the bones that make up your day, weekly routines are the backbone—they provide the support and structure that hold everything together. When you handle things like what's for dinner, prepping food, keeping up with laundry, mopping the floors, and figuring out carpool on a weekly instead of a daily basis, you free up a ton of mental energy. Instead of scrambling at the last minute, you already have a plan, and everything has its time and place. With a solid weekly routine, your daily life runs much more smoothly, and you can focus on what really matters—without feeling like you're constantly playing catch-up.

Examples of Keystone Weekly Routines

- **Weekly Planning Session:** This was addressed in chapter 8, when I encouraged you to pick a standing date in your calendar to do this weekly. Make this a routine and set aside time, typically at the beginning or end of the week, to review your calendar, plan your priorities, and set goals for the days ahead. A routine helps reduce decision fatigue and ensures you're clear on what's coming up.
- **Family Check-In:** After that planning session, schedule a time to connect with your family and/or partner to review everyone's schedules for the week. This helps avoid surprises and keeps communication clear. You can plan for those hidden to-dos that come with each item on your plan. Who's picking up Quincy from school? Who's taking back the Amazon returns? What time is dinner? It's a great way to make sure everyone is aligned and supported. This doesn't have to take a long time, but it's life-changing in reducing stress.

- **Meal Planning, Grocery Shopping, and Meal Prepping:** There's nothing worse than deciding what to make for dinner at 5 p.m. when you are exhausted. After you plan your week, take some time to plan a few simple meals (refer to the resource in the previous chapter for a simple meal rotation). Then select a time for grocery shopping and preparing meals for the week. It reduces daily stress and ensures you have everything you need to eat well without scrambling. It also saves time and helps maintain healthy habits.
- **Household Tasks:** Creating a weekly routine for chores like laundry, cleaning, and organizing keeps your home running smoothly. We do a Sunday Sweep—a quick whole-house, whole-family "sweep." When the kids were little, I set a twenty-minute timer and we got to work. I would clear the main space, while Scott would oversee and help the kids with the playroom, doing a quick wipe-down of their bathrooms, and picking up their bedrooms. Going into the week with a fresh space was helpful, and doing it weekly (with daily tidies each night) meant that, for the most part, keeping a clean home didn't become overwhelming. You might choose a specific day for laundry or a time block for decluttering each week. This can change in different seasons. Now that my kids are older, I do laundry twice a week. When they were little and spilling all the time, I did laundry daily. I used to say, "A load of laundry a day keeps the overwhelm away." Having some sort of routine helps you to not feel as overwhelmed. You aren't left wondering and feeling shame about when you did it last. You know it will get done again soon (maybe not in the length of

time the experts tell us to, but who died and made them the experts anyway?).

- **Self-Care Time:** Friend, repeat after me: Self-care is not selfish. If you have been told that, just know I have been told that too. But it's not selfish to fill your car with gas and get the oil changed, is it? I think self-care has been poorly marketed. Building in time for self-care, whether it's a workout, reading, or taking a long hot shower, helps you recharge and fill up so you can pour out throughout the week. Plus, I do my best thinking in the shower or on a walk (this book might not have happened without those).

Is there a keystone weekly routine that could simplify your life and save you some stress?

Think about what feels cumbersome right now. What small tweak could help make things smoother for you? When you think of routines, don't just stop at daily ones. Consider those things you do—even just once a week—that can set you up for success all week long. Whether it's planning meals, doing a family check-in, or setting aside time for self-care, these weekly routines are the backbone that helps everything else fall into place. By building these into your week, you'll find yourself with less stress, more energy, and more space for what matters most.

Consider those things you do—even just once a week—that can set you up for success all week long.

THE **POWER** OF ROUTINES

Remember that hair-frazzled morning at the beginning of summer? Well, that night Scott and I sat down with the kids to talk about the day ahead. We realized we needed to tweak some things to make our mornings smoother. The next morning wasn't perfect, but it was less bumpy. Little by little we tweaked our daily and weekly routines. We practiced our way to automation, eventually finding our groove.

I noticed my texts to friends shifted too. Instead of sending SOS messages about our crazy mornings, I was texting them about pool dates and get-togethers. It was such a relief to move from frantic energy to a more relaxed pace, thanks to a few simple tweaks.

Routines are tools, not the goal.

Routines will ebb and flow with the season of life you're in. What worked when I was single didn't work when I was newly married and in grad school. What worked when the kids were little doesn't look the same now, and that's okay. More routines don't necessarily mean better ones, and not every moment has to be planned out. The goal is to create a rhythm for right now that supports you, not one that stresses you out. Routines are tools, not the goal. They offer you the structure you need to reach your goals, and they should bend and flex as life happens.

As you reflect on your routines, ask yourself, *What matters most to me right now?* Start there. The rest will fall into place with a little practice, patience, and grace. And remember, your routine doesn't have to look like mine—or anyone else's. The key is finding what works for both you and your family in this season of life.

TIME BLOCKING

Time blocking is a powerful way to organize your week by setting aside specific chunks of time to focus on certain tasks. It lets you focus on one priority at a time, helping you streamline your daily and weekly routines.

For example, in my work life, I time block like this:

Monday is for social media planning and creating content.
Tuesday is all about podcasts—recording, interviewing, and uploading.
Wednesday I plan with my assistant and write emails.
Thursday is for bigger projects like product and printable creations.
Friday is dedicated to planning the upcoming week.

Time blocking works seamlessly with keystone weekly routines like planning, meal prep, or laundry by giving those routines a specific time and place in your schedule. Keystone weekly routines are the essential tasks you do each week to stay on track and reduce stress. By assigning tasks a time in your calendar, you free up mental energy, reduce decision fatigue, and ensure your most important routines are prioritized.

Time blocking isn't just for work—it can help simplify your life, home, and everything in between. Here's how you can start:

1. **Identify your key tasks.** List your recurring weekly tasks, such as meal planning, cleaning, or work-related tasks.
2. **Assign days or time blocks.** Group similar tasks together. For inspiration:

Monday: Laundry day
Tuesday: Vacuuming and mopping
Wednesday: Bathrooms
Thursday: Errands or big work projects
Friday: Planning for next week, including meal planning
Weekend: Grocery shopping, filling the car with gas, meal prepping

I keep a flexible time-blocked list on my desktop and tweak it weekly. It's structured, not rigid. Life happens, and that's okay. If you're new to this, start small. You'll love the relief of knowing when things will actually get done.

Part 4
Maintain the Momentum

10

IT DOESN'T HAVE TO BE FANCY

We looked in the mirror as my ninety-two-year-old grandmother tried on glasses. There were hundreds of options, but we narrowed them down to a few pairs. The tortoiseshell round ones were my favorite. They gave her a dignified look. To convince her, I sent a group text to our family to garner support for my choice. She looked at herself in the mirror and remarked, "They're too fancy." Then she grabbed a pair we'd yet to try, put them on, and announced, "These are it." Out of the hundreds of frames in the showroom, she picked the exact same pair she already owned.

I couldn't help but smile. This was my grandmother to a T. She knew what she liked, and she stuck with it. Her wardrobe was a rotation of the same basic outfits: slacks, a solid-color top, and, in the winter, a wool cardigan she'd had for decades—gifted by one of us, of course. She used to make the same meal every time we visited, a Minnesota classic: hamburger rice hot dish with corn and buttered

Wonder bread. Her table is where I learned it doesn't have to be fancy to feed your family. I loved that meal. It felt like a hug from my grandmother. It didn't matter that she served it repeatedly. We wanted her to.

In addition to her glasses and cardigan and hamburger meal, my grandmother also has a habit of keeping a five-gallon tub of ice cream in her freezer and eating one scoop every night (maybe that's her secret to a long life). Her floral and turquoise velvet furniture? She's had it since the sixties, though she no longer covers it with sheets when I visit. She's never been fancy, but she's always been friendly, generous, down-to-earth, and playful. Oh, how she's playful.

When I was fourteen, she pulled a pair of stilts out of her trunk and showed my sister and me how it was done. This same woman hopped on an inflatable inner tube in her sixties, gripping tight as my dad whipped the boat in high-speed turns. She got soaked when the tube submerged us, but she emerged from the water laughing, full of joy despite the chaos. That's who she was and still is—a woman who finds joy, even in the wild waves of life.

Over the years, she and my grandfather taught me more than just how to make gingersnap cookies, dial a rotary phone, and drive a tractor. They showed me that life doesn't have to be fancy to be fulfilling. A simple life, honoring what matters most to you, can be rich and deeply satisfying.

Life doesn't have to be fancy to be fulfilling.

When I visit her now, we sit together quietly, soaking in the moment. She hugs me and tells me how glad she is that I'm there. While others around the table grumble about dull forks, cold coffee, or politics, she remains steady, content, and joyful. She looks at photos on my phone and tells me it's the highlight of her day. She comments on the beautiful weather and the flowers and birds in the garden outside the window. As she nears the sunset of her life, she could easily join the chorus of complaints, but she chooses joy. She's finishing well, a living reminder that fulfillment doesn't come from extravagance or perfection.

My grandmother's ability to find happiness in the familiar, to maintain her playful spirit, and to stay content with what she has—these are lessons we can all learn from. In a world that constantly tells us we need more, my grandmother has shown me we can find joy in simplicity. Simple doesn't mean boring.

IT DOESN'T HAVE TO BE **FANCY** TO BE **FUN**

"Bring your flute for Christmas. We'll have a family band."

I was in sixth grade and had been playing the flute for approximately four months. My grandmother arranged chairs in the living room near those sheet-covered floral couches, and my grandfather made copies of the three holiday songs I barely knew. He dusted off my dad's old trumpet, my mom brought her flute, my grandmother shook a tambourine, and my little sister, Ellen, sang. Would we have earned a quarter if we played on a street corner? Probably not. But we ended each song with wide smiles and laughter. What fun!

I grew up in a family that amplified the fun in life. My mom sang silly songs, and my dad tickled us until we were gasping for breath, our stomachs sore from laughing. It wasn't about doing anything fancy; it was just about finding joy in everyday moments.

I've carried their example into adulthood and look for every opportunity to have fun. One Christmas several years ago, the song "Dominick the Donkey"[1] came on. In a burst of inspiration, I taught my family a spontaneous dance to go along with it. Much like that family band, it wasn't perfect, but it was *fun*. Now, every year, whenever that song plays, I force everyone to stop what they're doing and join me. My kids might be mortified that I'm sharing this secret, but I've already warned them—we're doing this dance at their weddings. Even the most reluctant participants end up laughing and joining in, because sometimes, fun just pulls you in.

How Do We Find Fun?

After I posted "How do you find fun?" on Instagram, I received a response that stopped me in my tracks: "I can't remember the last time I laughed." One SPL squad member went on to share, "I don't know how to have fun." That message stuck with me. Not everyone grew up with tickle fests or goofy songs, and maybe fun feels distant for you too. The temptation might be to go big—to book the concert tickets, plan a getaway, or fly in a hot-air balloon. But by now you know that fun doesn't have to be complicated or expensive.

Think back to what you've written in your gratitude journal—the little things that brought happiness and joy. Those moments are your clues. Maybe it's a cozy afternoon with your favorite book or sending funny memes to the group chat (I can confirm: very fun). Fun isn't reserved for elaborate plans. The things that spark joy in your heart are often the simple, everyday activities.

And remember that white space you made in your calendar, those Happiness Spaces? That's where fun can sneak in. When you've made room for less busyness, you've made room for more joy. You can pull out a game and play it on a clutter-free surface, or dance freely without tripping over toys or piles of laundry. When there's less to manage, there's more space for joy and fun to shine through. Life becomes lighter and full of possibilities.

Fun can also be revisiting what brought you joy as a child. Was it riding bikes, playing outside, or drawing? Those childlike activities are still a part of you. You don't need to be good at them. Just enjoy them, simply *because* they bring you joy. You're never too old to find fun again.

Forget What Others Think of Fun

You might be wondering, *What will people think of me?* I get it. But here's the thing: When I see someone dancing in the street or laughing out loud, I don't judge them. I smile and think, *Good for them! They're enjoying life.* It's inspiring. If someone judges you for having fun, maybe they just need a little more fun in their life.

Instead of asking, *What will others think of me?* try shifting your perspective to *I hope this joy is contagious.* Because it is! Our attitudes are contagious—they can spread in either a positive or negative way. When you let yourself enjoy life, you might just give someone else permission to do the same. The ripple effect of joy is powerful. When you embrace fun, you might be planting the seed for others to do the same.

The ripple effect of joy is powerful. When you embrace fun, you might be planting the seed for others to do the same.

Don't underestimate those small, silly moments. They matter more than we think. Simple fun has a way of waking us up, of turning ordinary days into vivid memories. Most of life fades in our minds over time. We forget what we wore, what we ate, even what we said. But fun? Fun helps us remember. I spent countless moments with my grandparents over the years, but the ones etched most deeply in my memory? They are the moments when we were laughing, playing, and having fun.

IT DOESN'T HAVE TO BE FANCY TO **FOSTER CONNECTION**

A parent commented after one of my kids' birthday parties, "My daughter had a blast, and it was simple." She was right, and it was on purpose. We angled a makeshift Slip 'N Slide down the side of our hill, using the largest tarp I could find at Walmart. The kids made two-ingredient sugar scrubs and topped the day off with ice-cream sundaes. The smiles were real, the laughter was loud, and the joy was genuine. And none of it required anything fancy.

This simplicity came after years of going all out because I thought I should—renting party spaces, hiring entertainment, trying to make everything Pinterest-perfect. But more often than not, those elaborate plans left me exhausted and distracted. And for what? A polished photo? A perfectly curated moment? Somewhere along the way, I realized I was missing the point. The more elaborate I made things, the more I lost sight of what mattered most: being present and connecting with the people I love.

In today's world, it's easy to feel like everything needs to be elevated, extra, or eventworthy. But some of life's most meaningful moments are incredibly simple. I got engaged in my pajamas on a Tuesday night and celebrated with a five-dollar bottle of champagne

TINY TWEAKS FOR EVERYDAY FUN

Let's inject some fun into your daily life. Remember, it doesn't have to be fancy, and it doesn't have to be reserved for special days. Here are some practical tweaks to amplify fun in your routines:

- Have dance parties while doing chores.
- Sing in the shower.
- Schedule regular game or movie nights with family or friends.
- Pick up a hobby that sparks your curiosity: painting, gardening, photography, or learning a new instrument.
- Engage in spontaneous acts of kindness: leaving kind notes, helping a neighbor.
- Go for a walk or hike and explore a new area.
- Try a DIY project or start a new collection of something you enjoy.
- Play board games or take up geocaching.

my roommate had in the fridge. It wasn't fancy, but it was perfect. It was real, heartfelt, and completely us. We live in a culture that often celebrates the elaborate. But sometimes in our effort to make things perfect, we miss out on the actual magic—being together.

You might remember that Harvard happiness study we talked about earlier in the book. It turns out, the people who live the happiest, healthiest lives aren't the ones with the most elaborate plans or packed social calendars; they're the ones who prioritize meaningful connection. I have learned it's not about how impressive your life looks from the outside; it's about how connected your heart feels on the inside.

Connection doesn't have to be complicated. My dad has always said the best gift in life is the gift of time—time to be with another person, fully present and engaged. And the older I get, the more I realize he's right (sorry it took me so long, Dad). The tweaks you've practiced throughout this book—setting standing dates, adding things to your calendar, leaving white space, and making room for rhythms—these are the quiet, powerful ways we create space for connection to grow. But even with the space cleared, connection doesn't always happen by accident. It takes courage and intention. It might mean flexing your fear muscle and being the one to reach out. This part can feel vulnerable. But often all it takes is a simple invitation—and connection begins to flow.

Connection doesn't have to be complicated.

DON'T LET **FANCY** LEAD TO REGRETS

Previously, we talked about perfectionism—the weight of pressure we put on ourselves to have it all together before we even begin. But what do we really want at the end of our lives? To have waited for the perfect moment? Or to have tried, learned, and grown, even when things didn't go as planned?

Research shows that we regret things we didn't do more than

the ones we tried and stumbled through.[2] What holds us back is the fear of failure and the pressure that everything has to be polished and perfect.

When I first had the idea to make the meal planner, I had zero design or business background. I hired a college student in design school to help with the layout, called dozens of places before someone agreed to work with me, and bought a secondhand printer and computer to get started. To this day, I still record podcasts in my bedroom closet.

I came across this quote one day: "Scrappiness is often misunderstood as a lack of resources, but in reality, it's the ability to make things happen with what you have." I don't know who said it, but I knew it described me. And maybe it describes you too. I've learned through the school of hard knocks and Google searches that resourcefulness is far more valuable than perfection. Mistakes? Yes, they'll happen. But I'm so glad I didn't let the idea of "fancy" stop me from starting. Because starting is what led me to this life—and to you.

Instead of getting stuck in fear or waiting for perfect, ask yourself, *What's one small thing I can do today to avoid the sting of regret tomorrow?* Maybe it's inviting a friend over, even if your house isn't perfectly clean. Maybe it's turning on some music and dancing, even if you're not a great dancer. Or jumping off the high dive with your son. Maybe it's grabbing a pair of metaphorical stilts, starting a family band, or simply taking an imperfect step toward something new. Because regret doesn't come from failing—it comes from not trying at all.

Regret doesn't come from failing—it comes from not trying at all.

Flex that fear muscle, sister. Make the tweak. Do the thing. This is your one life. I don't want you to miss out!

TWEAK YOUR WAY TO A HAPPY LIFE

When my world tipped off its axis all those years ago at my aunt's funeral, I realized I wasn't just living for myself but for those whose lives were cut short. That day changed me. It reminded me how fleeting and precious this life is—and that we don't get to choose how many days we have. But we do get to choose how we fill them.

This is not a dress rehearsal.

I've said it before and I will say it again: I don't simplify for simplification's sake. Sure, it's nice when things are easier, but the real purpose of tweaking my time, decluttering, and creating routines is to make room for happiness—to make space for connection. Intentionally creating margin in my life allows me to be fully present to savor the good moments. Life isn't just meant to be lived; it's meant to be enjoyed. No regrets! F-L-E-X that fear muscle, sister!

Celebrate the small wins and notice your progress. Talk to yourself the way you'd talk to someone you love. Speak gently and cheer loudly; after all, you're listening. Encourage others with genuine compliments and support. A heartfelt "You've got this!" can keep someone going, even on their hardest days. We've all made mistakes. We've all said things we regret or made decisions we wish we could take back. But when those memories pop up—whether it's that awkward college moment, a friendship that fell apart, or words that came out too fast—pause and breathe. Apologize when needed, forgive yourself, and know that every moment—especially the hardest ones—teaches us something. Living in the past will steal the joy available to you right now.

Focus on what you can do today. What's one small step, one tiny tweak, that points you in the direction you want to go? Crafting a life you love isn't about one big, sweeping leap—it's about the small, steady steps. It's the ordinary Tuesdays when you show up and choose joy again and again. These moments may not look fancy, but they are where the real magic happens.

If my grandparents taught me anything, it's that a rich, meaningful life doesn't have to be fancy—and it's not always easy either. They didn't have all the material wealth the world promises will make us happy. Life threw its share of challenges their way. But they kept going, focused on what truly mattered. And somehow, over a lifetime of ordinary days, they built something extraordinary. From where I sit, they were the richest people I knew.

Someday, if I'm lucky enough to grow old and gray like them, I hope I'll be sitting in a white rocking chair on my front porch, looking back on this one wild and beautiful life—the stressful moments faded to the background, and the sweet memories wrapped around me like a warm blanket.

I'll remember the laughter. The connection. The joy in the small things. That's the story I want to tell. The legacy I want to leave: *She tweaked her way to a life she loved.* And friend, that's the life I want for you too—simple, joyful, purposeful, and rich in all the ways that truly matter.

The good news? Tiny tweaks build powerful momentum—and you're already on your way.

Tweak your way to a life you love.

A LEGACY OF SIMPLICITY

Think of someone in your life—like my grandmother—who showed you that joy, fun, and connection don't have to be fancy to matter. What did their life teach you about what's truly important?

Now take it one step further: What's one area of your life the world has convinced you should be fancier or flashier—when deep down, you know it doesn't? **What tiny tweak could simplify it—on purpose**?

Maybe it's repeating the same dinner every Friday and calling it tradition.

Maybe it's singing the silly song, starting the dance party, or pulling out the "family band" instruments—just because it brings joy.

Let that one tweak be your reminder: It doesn't have to be fancy to be fun, connected, or fulfilling. Simplicity makes space for what really matters.

REFLECT ON THIS:

- Who in your life has modeled this kind of simple, meaningful living?
- What did their life teach you that you want to carry forward?
- What's one small way you can embrace that legacy this week by choosing simple on purpose?

11

TWEAKS TO MAINTAIN MOMENTUM

One night, I pulled into the driveway after an endless day of meetings. The sun was long gone, and my firstborn baby boy was fast asleep in his bed. I sat in the car and wept.

I had missed another bedtime.

This wasn't what I wanted.

Just months before he was born, I had donned a cap and gown in front of our family's lake home, too pregnant to walk the stage at graduation. I was on the path to accomplishing all the goals I had mapped out for years: Become an elementary school principal, then eventually a superintendent. But from the first moment I held my son in my arms, everything shifted. I no longer wanted the path I had been chasing—I just wanted to be home, with him.

A few months later, I turned in my resignation letter. Just like that, my jam-packed calendar emptied. The Outlook calendar that once buzzed with meetings and reminders now stared back at me—blank.

I traded business casual for an old T-shirt and stretched-out sweatpants. I stopped showering every day. With my son perched on my hip and my hair in yesterday's messy bun, I wandered the house, wondering, *What now?*

Motherhood was deeply purposeful, and I didn't regret making this big life change. But in this brand-new season, where the structure of the familiar evaporated, I found myself untethered. I missed the clarity of a schedule, the markers of productivity I had grown used to. So I opened my laptop and stared at my Outlook calendar, trying to bring some shape to the day ahead. I wanted to feel grounded again. But as I stared at the blinking cursor, I was left with the question, *What does a stay-at-home mom even schedule?*

9:00 a.m.: Change poopy diaper
10:00 a.m.: Load laundry
11:00 a.m.: Serve lunch
12:00 p.m.: Nap time (for my son . . . and me)

As I sat there staring at my list, it hit me: This is what I had wanted. I had longed for this slower pace, this time with my son. Yet now that I was in it, I didn't know how to show up in this new season with the same intention and drive I'd once poured into my career. I was physically present, but mentally, I'd checked out and was just going through the motions.

That's when I remembered Admiral William H. McRaven's famous commencement speech, the one I still receive from friends and family who know how deeply it resonated with me. He said, "If you want to change the world, start off by making your bed."[1] His message was simple but powerful: Start your day by making your bed, because small actions build momentum and set the tone for everything that follows.

Small actions build momentum and set the tone for everything that follows.

It sounds almost trivial, but making your bed, or doing a small task like it, sets the tone for the day. It gives you a win right out of the gate—a sign to yourself that you're showing up on purpose. So I tried it. I made my bed. Nothing fancy—I just pulled up the comforter and set the pillows back up, but it felt good—like I had done something. To this day, when I'm feeling unmotivated or stuck, McRaven's words come to mind, and they give me the push I need. It's like the first pedal of the bike. Once you start, it's easier to keep going.

And I'm not the only one. I asked some other women in our SPL community how they show up well for their days, and here's what they said:

"Always contacts and a bra, followed up with a prayer and devotion time." —Elizabeth

"Get dressed, and a little makeup says I mean business." —Amy

"Start with a to-do list and a little dancing." —Stacy

"I do the same routine whether working from my home office or going to work. I also like to play background music. It helps me focus and get motivated." —Angel

"I wash my hair every morning." —Catherine

These small but intentional actions may seem like no big deal, but the *bed-making moments* are the tiny tweaks that shift your

What small, meaningful action could you commit to each morning that says, "I'm here, I'm awake, and I'm showing up"?

mindset from surviving to showing up. What's your bed-making moment? What small, meaningful action could you commit to each morning that says, "I'm here, I'm awake, and I'm showing up," no matter how chaotic life gets or how lost you feel? It doesn't have to be complicated or time-consuming—it just needs to matter to you.

As you think about what that morning moment might be, remember that these small actions aren't small at all. They are the building blocks of something larger. They're the momentum you need. One tiny tweak can shift the whole rhythm of your day or completely change your attitude. And tiny tweaks don't have to be difficult to make a difference and to keep the momentum going. Think of them like a lever—a small move that creates a big shift—to help everything else align with the kind of life you actually want to live.

YOU DON'T NEED TO GO BIG

When we're making changes that we hope have lasting impact, we don't have to "go big or go home." The world often tells us we need bigger goals, bolder moves, and flashier everything, but what if the real win isn't in the grand gestures? What if it's in the small, consistent actions we take each day—the ones we actually stick with?

When we show up for the day, we show up for life. This life, handpicked for you, is like a tapestry—woven moment by moment.

SMALL ACTIONS,
AWARENESS, AND
ACCOUNTABILITY
HELP YOU
KEEP MOVING
FORWARD.

Yes, there are knots and tangles, and some days may feel like it's all unraveling. But those small stitches, those tiny moments we embrace, hold it all together.

Remember my story about crying in the hallway after Quincy came home? I was exhausted, overwhelmed, and unsure how to keep going. In that quiet moment, I didn't overhaul my life. I leaned in to the little things—the small tweaks I could manage, even in the chaos. And now, all these years later, I see how all those intentional tweaks added up—not to perfection but to a life I treasure.

HOW TO **MAINTAIN THE MOMENTUM** WHEN LIFE FEELS HARD

She had me at the navy-striped shirt she was wearing. I've always loved navy stripes, and I just knew this woman I spotted at the library would be a kindred spirit. She had two kids the same ages as mine and was sitting alone. I gave her my number, and that navy-striped gal became my best friend.

When life feels overwhelming or different from what we expected, it's the small actions that help us keep moving forward.

We were inseparable in those early years of motherhood, spending hours together while our kids played. But as time passed, things changed. Our kids went to different schools, I moved farther away, and, eventually, our friendship fell apart. It was painful and hard to accept. Through that experience, I learned that seasons shift, and no matter how much we want to hold on, we can't. But when life feels overwhelming or different from what we expected, it's the small actions that help us keep moving forward.

There will be days when showing up feels impossible—when you're too tired, too stressed, too heartbroken, or stretched too thin to give much. That's when the little things matter most. Making my bed felt pointless at first, but it gave me a sense of accomplishment and shifted my outlook for the day. It gave me a small win.

Excuses will come. Life will absolutely get in the way. But, as my friend Alli Worthington said, "The breakthrough you want is in the work you're avoiding."[2] Every time we choose to show up—especially in the tough moments—we build resilience and reinforce our progress. So, when life feels heavy, when everything in you wants to shut down and you feel a little (or a lot) lost, remember that small steps—tiny tweaks—are still steps forward.

MOMENTUM DOESN'T REQUIRE **PERFECTION**

A few years ago I started walking regularly, but on busy days I skipped it, because if I didn't have time for the full routine, what was the point? I had fallen into the trap so many of us know well: *If I can't do it perfectly, I won't do it at all.* But then I realized how much I was missing out on—all those little pockets of time I could've been walking, clearing my head, and taking a deep breath. That's when it hit me: *Some is better than none.*

This small tweak—allowing "some" to be enough—was a turning point. I let go of the idea that consistency required perfection. Doing "some" gave me the benefits I'd been craving without the pressure of perfection I'd been placing on myself. My mood lifted, and I felt accomplished just for doing *something*.

I shared this idea—*some is better than none*—on Instagram, and someone messaged me: "My all-or-nothing thinking kept me from building habits in the past, but today I walked a few blocks, and I'm glad I did."

When we insist on perfection, we miss out on progress.

Same, sister. Same!

Perfectionism doesn't show up just in our fitness goals. It sneaks into all areas of our life. We hesitate to apply for a job because we're not 100 percent qualified. We avoid reaching out to friends because we don't have hours to catch up. We skip inviting people over because the house isn't spotless.

But Voltaire said it best: "Perfect is the enemy of good."[3] When we insist on perfection, we miss out on progress. We delay action, waiting for the perfect moment or perfect conditions, and in doing so, we often miss the good that's right in front of us.

Ask yourself, *Where am I holding back because I feel like it needs to be perfect? What would change if I embraced "some is better than none"?* Let's let go of perfect. Let's keep showing up consistently with open hands. That's where growth lives.

WHEN **COMPARISON DERAILS** YOUR MOMENTUM

One day, I hopped on my regular call with my friend and business coach, Alli Worthington. I had that familiar pit-in-my-stomach feeling—like I was falling behind. I had just finished a scrolling session. You know the kind—where everyone's winning. Someone's on a dream vacation, another just ran a marathon, and someone else just renovated their kitchen and it looks like it came straight out of a magazine. Meanwhile, I was sitting there wondering if I was doing enough, keeping up. Ever felt that way?

When I shared this feeling, Alli asked me, "When do you tend to compare yourself the most?" That question hit me like a ton of bricks. I realized comparison creeps in when I'm already feeling insecure.

And that's exactly what comparison does—it stalls us. It whispers that someone else is further along, better equipped, or more successful. It makes us question the small, intentional steps we've faithfully been taking. Comparison kills momentum by convincing us our progress isn't enough. At its core, comparison stems from the belief that there isn't enough success, happiness, or opportunity to go around. But that's simply not true. I remind myself often that "her" win doesn't equal my loss. There's more than enough good available for everyone.

Social media amplifies the problem. It gives us constant access to the highlight reels of other people's lives, and before we know it, we're stuck in a cycle of measuring our lives against someone else's. If we're not careful, comparison can undo the momentum we've worked so hard to build. But here's the truth: You're not behind. You're on your own path. And the only thing that matters is that you keep going.

If we're not careful, comparison can undo the momentum we've worked so hard to build.

So if you're in a season where everyone else seems to be

TINY TWEAKS TO OVERCOME COMPARISON

Awareness is powerful. When you notice comparison creeping in, try one of these tweaks:

1. **Unplug and take a break.** Social media is a breeding ground for comparison. When you start to compare, put your phone away. Consider unfollowing a person whom you constantly compare yourself to. If that's not possible, mute them (they won't know). We can't help but compare what we see. Make it harder to see.
2. **Write in your gratitude journal.** Gratitude is a powerful antidote to comparison. When you record what you're grateful for, you focus on the good in your life. It helps you see that abundance exists, not just in someone else's life but in yours too.
3. **Track your progress.** Instead of measuring your success against others', track your personal growth. Celebrate the small wins, even if they seem insignificant. Progress celebrates how far you've come.
4. **Celebrate others without comparing.** When someone else succeeds, celebrate it. Send a genuine compliment—a DM, a text, even a snail-mail note. When you celebrate others, you connect—and remember there's enough success for everyone.
5. **Reflect and reframe.** When comparison creeps in, ask yourself, *Am I measuring my success by someone else's standards? What's going well in my life right now?* These questions help you shift focus back to your own journey.

These tiny tweaks help you ditch comparison and celebrate the good in your own life. Remember, *some is better than none*, and small steps forward are still progress—especially when you're focused on your own path, not someone else's.

sprinting while you're walking, keep walking. One small, meaningful step at a time. Because your journey wasn't meant to look like anyone else's.

AWARENESS IS A SUPERPOWER

Over the past few years, I've been working with a therapist who has helped me unpack some of the thoughts and patterns that were quietly sabotaging my peace. For the longest time, I was fumbling around in the dark with these heavy feelings—guilt, doubt, overwhelm—bumping into them but not knowing how to name them, much less navigate them.

Then one day, as I sat in my therapist's office, it felt like she'd flipped on a flashlight in that dark room. Suddenly I could see what had been tripping me up: limiting beliefs and silent expectations that had quietly been stalling my momentum. It reminded me of that moment from chapter 1, when my grandma thought she was drowning and my mom calmly reminded her, "Stand up." That's what awareness does. It helps us see clearly again. It reminds us that we're not failing—we might just be disoriented.

That moment was powerful. Simply being aware of these internal pitfalls gave me a way forward. Guilt, for example, can feel like a heavy anchor, dragging me down with reminders of what I haven't done—like choosing my phone over unplugging and being present, or focusing on the 1 percent that went wrong (like forgetting Quincy's Super Reader Day) instead of the 99 percent that went right. Negativity distorts everything. It seems like nothing is working, even when that's not true.

What's the tweak? Awareness is our superpower. By shining a light on these feelings, we can arm ourselves with truths that keep us moving forward. Instead of drowning in guilt, we can remind ourselves, *I am doing my best, and that's enough.* When negativity threatens to take over, we can pause and look for three bright spots from our day, no matter how small. When self-doubt creeps in, we can get curious instead of critical. We can ask a friend, therapist, or spouse for perspective, or simply step back and ask, *What else might be true here?* And when we feel stuck, we can always come back to this question: *What's a tweak I can make?*

Awareness doesn't erase the hard, but it helps us reset and keep going.

And when things still feel challenging? One of the most freeing things my therapist ever told me is this: "Bad moments don't have to mean bad days." This simple reminder has helped me more times than I can count. Awareness doesn't erase the hard, but it helps us reset and keep going.

ACCOUNTABILITY IS YOUR FRIEND

After my first book proposal was rejected, I was given the name of a writing coach, Ann. I hired her, and she helped me bravely try again. I can confidently say that I am a better writer because of her guidance. Because of all I learned from her, I decided to invest in a business coach—Alli, whom you've already met in these pages. One day on yet another call, I told her I thought I needed to see a therapist. Without skipping a beat, she said, "If you're willing to invest in your business, why wouldn't you invest in tending to your soul?" That question hit me hard—and gently pushed me to seek the support I truly needed. *Accountability* became my 2024 word of the year. That was the year I finally embraced and found accountability.

You can only get so far on your own.

That was the year I finally learned this powerful truth: You can only get so far on your own. (It took me forty-one years to understand this.) Accountability used to intimidate me. I used to bristle at the thought of it. It challenged the last bit of that "I've got this" mentality. But the truth? I don't have this. Not on my own. And I'm actually thankful to have learned that. Letting others speak into your life isn't weakness—it's wisdom. That's what you've done by picking up this book. You were ready to let someone walk beside you. That's what accountability does. It invites others in—people who can cheer you on, challenge you, and gently speak truth when your thoughts start to spiral.

My friends Ann, Alli, and Elizabeth, along with others, are those people for me. Their insights often come with a little "ouch," but they stretch me in all the right ways. Their words often linger, so when I hit a roadblock—like guilt, negativity, or self-doubt—I don't hear the old lies. I hear their voices reminding me of what's true.

Here's my question for you: Who can you invite into your life to help you maintain the momentum you've built by making tiny tweaks? Find the ones who will lock arms with you and shine a light on what you can't see. Find the people who, when you think you're drowning, will gently call out, like my mom did for my grandma, "Stand up."

And if my words have lingered in your heart—even just a little—I hope they're the ones you hear when doubt or fear creeps in. You don't have to do this alone. Trust yourself. Keep going. The next tweak is always one step away.

KEEP GOING ONE TWEAK AT A **TIME**

Have you ever run a 400-meter race? I have—once. I was assigned to run it for the sixth-grade district track meet. I remember standing at the starting line, butterflies buzzing in my stomach, semiconfident I could handle just one lap around the track. How hard could it be? Here's the thing you need to know about the 400-meter race: It *looks* short on paper, but when you're in it, it feels long. Your legs start burning. Your lungs too. You think to yourself, *This shouldn't be this hard.* But it is.

Halfway through, I wanted to stop, losing momentum. I started comparing. *She's ahead. I'm falling behind. Why is this so much easier for everyone else?* I vowed right then and there I'd never run a 400-meter race again, and I can confidently say I've kept that vow. But in many ways, that race reminds me of life. On paper, it might not look like it should be that hard. But when you're in the middle of it? Your energy fades. Your doubts flare up. You lose your rhythm and start looking left and right. That's when it's easiest to stall out. To think you need a big reset or a brand-new plan (or never to run the 400 again). It's easy to feel like you're failing when really you're just in the middle of something. It's easy to lose momentum and forget you're still in the race.

Those middle moments when you're really in it—stretching yourself, facing fears, trying to grow—are where momentum matters most. And momentum doesn't come from perfection. It comes from small, purposeful shifts—one tiny tweak at a time. It takes faith. It takes trust. It takes letting go of the idea that progress should be linear, or that you'll always be able to see the finish line. Sometimes you can't. You don't have to know all the steps ahead. What you need is a tweak—a small, intentional action to help you show up to your life, even when it feels uncertain.

You don't have to know all the steps ahead. What you need is a tweak—a small, intentional action to help you show up to your life, even when it feels uncertain.

Tiny tweaks have carried me through motherhood, through friendship transitions, and through the joys and challenges of adoption. Even when I wasn't sure what came next, I kept making the tweak to take the next step. Sometimes it was a short walk to clear my mind; other times it was making my bed to create order or letting go of the need to be perfect. These were small steps that helped me move forward.

When you find yourself in your next "400-meter race" in life, remember: Sometimes what keeps you going isn't your legs—it's the people in the stands. The ones cheering you on. The ones shouting, "You've got this!" when you're ready to quit. That's what support does. That's what grace does. That's what truth does—especially when it's louder than the lies in your head.

So when the race of life feels long . . .

When the curve throws you off . . .

When you feel unsure, behind, or off course . . .

Pause. Breathe. Refocus.

Make the tweak you need to keep going. And at the end of the day, it isn't really about the finish line—it's about who you become along the way. You don't have to do it perfectly. You just need to keep showing up faithfully. And that's what momentum really is.

TWEAK YOUR WAY TO A **LIFE YOU LOVE**

You've made it to the end of this book, but really, this is just the beginning. Everything we've explored together—from gratitude and routines to simplicity and courage—was never about adding more. It's about learning to live with intention and tweaking your way to a life you truly love.

Gratitude helps you notice the beauty that's already there. Learning how you use your time makes space for what matters most. Flexing your fear muscle—being willing to try even when you feel unsure—will carry you forward when you feel stuck. And knowing life doesn't have to be fancy to be full? That changes everything.

Along the way, we've discovered that happiness isn't found in hustle or perfection. It's found in gratitude and presence—in meaningful relationships, time in nature, small acts of kindness, a sense of purpose, and savoring the moment right in front of you. You don't have to chase a brand-new life. You can tweak the beautiful one you already have—one small shift at a time. That's the heart of it, really: A tweaked life is a happy life.

As you make these tiny tweaks, I hope you'll pause to celebrate your wins, no matter how small. Jot a note in your gratitude journal, share a high five with a friend, or simply take a breath and notice the goodness. These moments are more than milestones—they're reminders that your life is starting to reflect what matters most. When Quincy finally leaned in for a hug, when I left my phone behind and felt untethered, when a friend reached out just because—those were my breadcrumbs. They told me I was on the right path. You'll find your own. Keep looking. Each of those moments, each quiet act of resilience, adds up to a life that reflects your values, your heart, and your hope.

A happy life isn't built overnight. It's built slowly—tweak by tweak. Keep showing up. Keep learning, even when it's messy. Take the scenic route when you can. Roll down the windows. Let your hair blow in the breeze. Pull over for pie. Snap the picture. Laugh out loud. Don't just manage your life—live it.

Here I am, pom-poms in hand, high kicking and shouting at the top of my lungs:

> "Tiny changes, one by one.
> Keep on tweaking, have some fun.
> Simplify to make life bright—
> That's the way to joy and light!"

If no one has told you lately, hear it now from me: Good job! You've made it this far. I'm proud of you. I see the invisible load you carry. I see your effort and your courage. Now go—go live that beautifully tweaked, joy-filled life you're envisioning. I'll be cheering you on the whole way.

MAINTAIN THE MOMENTUM QUESTIONS

As you reflect on your journey through this book, take a moment to consider the following questions. These prompts are designed to help you internalize the key concepts and apply them to your daily life. Whether you're looking to embrace happiness, find your next tweak, or simply maintain your momentum, these questions will guide you toward meaningful actions and insights.

1. What makes you happy in your day-to-day life?
2. Where do you need to flex your fear muscle?
3. What tiny space do you need to declutter?
4. What tweak can you make to unplug and let go of digital distractions?
5. What tweak can you make to plan for happiness in your week?
6. What routine can you tweak to automate what matters?
7. What's a small win to celebrate?
8. Where do you need accountability in your life? Who can you reach out to for support when you feel like you're losing momentum?
9. What brings you joy? When was the last time you felt truly fulfilled?

ACKNOWLEDGMENTS

I am deeply grateful to so many people who have invested in me over the years and in this book.

I want to thank my literary agent, Jenni Burke, for taking a chance on me as a first-time writer. Your belief in my vision and your invaluable support, along with your incredible team at Illuminate, made this journey possible.

A heartfelt thanks to Ann Kroeker, my writing coach, who not only encouraged me to be brave enough to throw out my initial proposal when it was rejected but also guided me with wisdom and enthusiasm throughout the process. Your support and cheerleading were instrumental in helping me find my voice and shape this book. I am a better writer for knowing you.

Kara Mannix and your talented team at Zondervan, thank you for seeing the potential in this book and for your unwavering dedication in bringing it to life. Your expertise and belief in the project were crucial to its completion.

Thank you to my friends and extended family, my early readers who gave me some tough love so I could make this book even better for the reader. We never get where we are going alone. Many have invested in me, and I am grateful for your friendship and encouragement.

Solon, Vera, Lucille, and Quincy—my kids—you are the greatest gifts God has given Dad and me. You are the reason I pursue a simple and purposeful life. Thank you for being my biggest cheerleaders. Your prayers and encouragement made the sacrifices worth it. I hope you see you can achieve your dreams, even if you fall flat on your face at first. Get back up and try again. Dreams take work, but they matter when you invest in others with the gifts you are given.

Scott, my great love and rock, thanks for listening to me read this a gazillion times and not letting me quit when I wanted to. You are the wind in my sails and the constant guide keeping me on course. Your support means more than words can express. I definitely married up!

My sister, Ellen, thank you for making me feel like the best big sister, despite my occasional bossiness. Your notes, love, and encouragement, both daily and hourly, have been a source of immense strength.

Mom and Dad, the locket you gave me at graduation, which read, "The world is yours," has been a guiding reminder of your unwavering support. Thank you for giving me the opportunities to stretch my wings and find resilience, and thank you for catching me when I fell. I am who I am because of your love, and for that I am forever grateful.

Grandma and Grandpa Wetherbee, thank you for being the inspiration and example for what a simple and purposeful life looks like. This is your legacy I pass on to others. I miss you, but the memories we shared are tucked deep in my heart. Save me a bowl of soft-serve ice cream in heaven!

Lastly, Jesus, my rock and savior, this book is a testament to Your guidance and grace. You rescued me at twenty-one and changed the trajectory of my life. I can never repay You for the gift of eternity, but my hope is to honor You with my whole heart and to steward the gifts You've given me to the best of my ability. You are the best tweak I've ever made. I give this to You produced by faith, motivated by love, and inspired by hope (1 Thessalonians 1:3). May this work glorify and honor You.

NOTES

Introduction

1. "Happiness Among Americans Dips to Five-Decade Low," UChicago News, June 16, 2020, https://news.uchicago.edu/story/happiness-among-americans-dips-five-decade-low.

Chapter 1: Mind Your Mindset

1. Emily P. Freeman, *The Next Right Thing*, podcast, accessed August 8, 2024, https://emilypfreeman.com/podcast/.
2. *Merriam-Webster*, s.v., "tweak," accessed April 11, 2025, https://www.merriam-webster.com/dictionary/tweak.
3. Stephen R. Covey, *The 7 Habits of Highly Effective People: Powerful Lessons in Personal Change* (Free Press, 1989), 287.

Chapter 2: What Makes You Happy?

1. Luc Olinga, "Loneliness Is Quietly Killing America (and the West)," Medium, January 14, 2024, https://medium.com/@lucolinga72/loneliness-is-killing-the-us-and-the-west-198a1ce50926.
2. "New APA Poll: One in Three Americans Feels Lonely Every Week," American Psychiatric Association, January 30, 2024, https://www.psychiatry.org/news-room/news-releases/new-apa-poll-one-in-three-americans-feels-lonely-e.
3. John Cacioppo and Louise Hawkley, "Perceived Social Isolation and Cognition," *Trends in Cognitive Sciences*, vol. 13, no. 10 (2009): 447–454, https://doi.org/10.1016/j.tics.2009.06.005.
4. "Harvard Study of Adult Development," Harvard Medical School, accessed August 3, 2024, https://www.adultdevelopmentstudy.org.
5. "Shaq Opens Up About His Divorce and His Only Regrets: Penny Hardaway and Kobe Bryant," *The Pivot Podcast*, April 22, 2022, https://youtu.be/m3vozVLCYwo?si=jrr85b3hUvLrA5zt.
6. Julianne Holt-Lunstad et al., "Social Relationships and Mortality Risk: A Meta-Analytic Review," *PLOS Medicine*, vol. 7, no. 7 (2010): e1000316, https://doi.org/10.1371/journal.pmed.1000316.

7. Laura Tremaine, *The Life Council: 10 Friends Every Woman Needs* (Zondervan, 2023), 124.
8. Commonly attributed to Confucius or used in motivational literature.
9. Ashley Abramson, "Seven Types of Rest to Help Restore Your Body's Energy," American Psychological Association, May 6, 2025, https://www.apa.org/topics/mental-health/seven-rest-types.
10. "How Much Sleep Do You Really Need?," National Sleep Foundation, October 1, 2020, https://www.thensf.org/how-many-hours-of-sleep-do-you-really-need/.
11. Eric Suni and John DeBanto, "How Sleep Works: Understanding the Science of Sleep," SleepFoundation.org, updated December 22, 2023, https://www.sleepfoundation.org/how-sleep-works/.
12. "The Health Benefits of Sunshine (and How Much You Need per Day)," Cleveland Clinic, February 20, 2025, https://health.clevelandclinic.org/how-much-sunshine-you-need-daily.
13. "Adult Activity: An Overview," U.S. Centers for Disease Control and Prevention, December 20, 2023, https://www.cdc.gov/physical-activity-basics/guidelines/adults.html.
14. Kirsten Weir, "Nurtured by Nature," *Monitor on Psychology*, April 1, 2020, vol. 51, no. 3 (2020), https://www.apa.org/monitor/2020/04/nurtured-nature.

Chapter 3: What Matters Most to You?

1. Charles R. Swindoll, *The Grace Awakening* (Word Publishing, 1990), 204.
2. Ann Voskamp, *One Thousand Gifts: A Dare to Live Fully Right Where You Are* (Zondervan, 2011).
3. Greg McKeown, *Essentialism: The Disciplined Pursuit of Less* (Crown Business, 2014).
4. Annie Dillard, *The Writing Life* (Harper & Row, 1989), 32.

Chapter 4: Flex Your Fear Muscle

1. Marie Forleo, *Everything Is Figureoutable* (Portfolio/Penguin, 2019), 96.
2. Forleo, *Everything Is Figureoutable,* 113.
3. Rachel Platten, "Fight Song," track 5 on *Wildfire*, Columbia Records, 2015.
4. Shania Twain, "Man! I Feel Like a Woman!," track 8 on *Come on Over*, Mercury Nashville, 1997.
5. Sara Bareilles, "Brave," track 1 on *The Blessed Unrest*, Epic Records, 2013.
6. Pitbull feat. Christina Aguilera, "Feel This Moment," track 4 on *Global Warming*, Mr. 305, Polo Grounds Music, 2012.
7. Scott Edwards, "Dancing and the Brain," Harvard Medical School, Winter 2015, https://hms.harvard.edu/news-events/publications-archive/brain/dancing-brain.
8. Eldon L. Ham, *All the Babe's Men: Baseball's Greatest Home Run Seasons and How They Changed America* (Potomac Books, 2013), 86.
9. Alison Lumbatis, *The Alison Lumbatis Show* podcast, https://alisonlumbatis.com.
10. "How to Find Your Fashion Style & Simplify Getting Dressed with Alison Lumbatis from Outfit Formulas," *Simple Purposeful Living Podcast with Erin Port*, episode 49, Podbean, April 2, 2024, https://erinqe.podbean.com/e/how-to-find-your-fashion-style-simplify-getting-dressed-with-alison-lumbatis-from-outfit-formulas/.

Chapter 5: Clear the Clutter

1. Joshua Becker, "21 Surprising Statistics That Reveal How Much Stuff We Actually Own," Becoming Minimalist, accessed May 21, 2018, https://www.becomingminimalist.com/clutter-stats/.
2. Marie Kondo, *The Life-Changing Magic of Tidying Up: The Japanese Art of Decluttering and Organizing* (Ten Speed Press, 2014), 182.

3. Francine Jay, *The Joy of Less: A Minimalist Guide to Declutter, Organize, and Simplify* (Chronicle Books, 2016), 120.

Chapter 6: Ditch the Digital Distractions

1. Manisha Saini, "New Screen Time Statistics [2025]: How Much Time We Spend on Screens?," Cropink, April 10, 2025, https://cropink.com/screen-time-statistics.
2. Anna Lembke, "Digital Addictions Are Drowning Us in Dopamine," *The Wall Street Journal*, August 13, 2021, https://www.wsj.com/health/wellness/digital-addictions-are-drowning-us-in-dopamine-11628861572?mod=Searchresults_pos1.
3. Gloria Mark et al., "The Cost of Interrupted Work: More Speed and Stress," *Proceedings of the SIGCHI Conference on Human Factors in Computing Systems* (ACM, 2008), 107–10, https://doi.org/10.1145/1357054.1357072.
4. Anne Lamott, *Almost Everything: Notes on Hope* (Riverhead Books, 2018), 67.
5. Hannah Brencher, *The Unplugged Hours: Cultivating a Life of Presence in a Digitally Connected World* (Zondervan, 2024).
6. Erin Port, host, *Simple Purposeful Living*, podcast, episode 72, September 17, 2024, "The Unplugged Hours with Hannah Brencher," Cloud10, https://podcasts.apple.com/us/podcast/the-unplugged-hours-with-hannah-brencher/id1685965308?i=1000669808585.
7. Jean M. Twenge, "Have Smartphones Destroyed a Generation?," *The Atlantic*, September 2017, https://www.theatlantic.com/magazine/archive/2017/09/has-the-smartphone-destroyed-a-generation/534198/; Matthew A. Killingsworth and Daniel T. Gilbert, "A Wandering Mind Is an Unhappy Mind," *Science*, vol. 330, no. 6006 (2010): 932, https://doi.org/10.1126/science.1192439.
8. Deirdre Fitzpatrick, "'Dying to Ask' Podcast: 5 Reasons Why You Need a Digital Sunset," KCRA Channel 3, updated March 6, 2025, https://www.kcra.com/article/dying-to-ask-podcast-5-reasons-why-you-need-a-digital-sunset/63904547.
9. Jonathan Trotter, "Why You Should Put Your Phone Away," Gottman Institute, last updated May 15, 2025, https://www.gottman.com/blog/put-your-phone-away-enjoy-unstructured-moments/.
10. Brittany Wood et al., "Light Level and Duration of Exposure Determine the Impact of Self-Luminous Tablets on Melatonin Suppression," *Applied Ergonomics*, vol. 44, no. 2 (2013): 237–40, https://doi.org/10.1016/j.apergo.2012.07.008.; Charles A. Czeisler, "Perspective: Casting Light on Sleep Deficiency," *Nature* 497, S13 (2013), https://doi.org/10.1038/497S13a.
11. Anne Lamott, *Almost Everything*, 67.

Chapter 7: Make the Most of Your Minutes

1. Cassie Holmes, *Happier Hour: How to Beat Distraction, Expand Your Time, and Focus on What Matters Most* (Gallery Books, 2022), 9.
2. Sonja Lyubomirsky, *The How of Happiness: A New Approach to Getting the Life You Want* (Penguin Press, 2007), 35.
3. The following quote is largely attributed to Mark Twain: "If it's your job to eat a frog, it's best to do it first thing in the morning. And if it's your job to eat two frogs, it's best to eat the biggest one first."
4. Brian Tracy, *Eat That Frog!: 21 Great Ways to Stop Procrastinating and Get More Done in Less Time*, (Berrett-Koehler Publishers, 2017).
5. "Why Multitasking Doesn't Work," Cleveland Clinic, March 10, 2021, https://health.clevelandclinic.org/science-clear-multitasking-doesnt-work.

6. Greg McKeown, *Effortless: Make It Easier to Do What Matters Most* (Crown Currency, 2021), 5.
7. Dan Zakay and Richard Block, "Prospective and Retrospective Duration Judgments: An Executive-Control Perspective," *Acta Neurobiologiae Experimentalis*, vol. 64, no. 3 (2004): 319–28, https://doi.org/10.55782/ane-2004-1516.
8. Brigid Schulte, *Overwhelmed: Work, Love, and Play When No One Has the Time* (Sarah Crichton Books, 2014).

Chapter 8: Plan for What Matters

1. Cal Newport, "Deep Habits: Plan Your Week in Advance," *Study Hacks* (blog), August 8, 2014, https://calnewport.com/deep-habits-plan-your-week-in-advance/.
2. Steve Jobs, quoted in "Voices of Innovation: Steve Jobs," *Businessweek*, October 11, 2004, https://www.bloomberg.com/news/articles/2004-10-10/voices-of-innovation-steve-jobs.
3. Jennifer Lynn Barnes, (@jenlynnbarnes), "One time, I was at a Q&A with Nora Roberts . . ." Twitter (now X), January 22, 2020, https://x.com/jenlynnbarnes/status/1220182162118451200.
4. Henry David Thoreau, *Letters to Harrison Gray Otis Blake*, in *Great Short Works of Henry David Thoreau*, ed. Wendell Glick (Harper & Row, 1982), 100, https://www.walden.org/wp-content/uploads/2016/08/LettersBlake.pdf.
5. Arianna Huffington, *Thrive: The Third Metric to Redefining Success and Creating a Life of Well-Being, Wisdom, and Wonder* (Harmony, 2014).

Chapter 9: Automate What Matters

1. James Clear, *Atomic Habits: An Easy and Proven Way to Build Good Habits & Break Bad Ones* (Avery, 2018), 40.
2. S.J. Scott, *Habit Stacking: 127 Small Changes to Improve Your Health, Wealth, and Happiness* (Oldtown Publishing, 2017), 156.
3. Greg McKeown, *Essentialism: The Disciplined Pursuit of Less* (Crown Business, 2014), 157.
4. Phillippa Lally et al., "How Are Habits Formed: Modelling Habit Formation in the Real World," *European Journal of Social Psychology*, vol. 40, no. 6 (2010): 998–1009, https://doi.org/10.1002/ejsp.674.

Chapter 10: It Doesn't Have to Be Fancy

1. Lou Monte, "Dominick the Donkey," written by Ray Allen, Sam Saltzberg, and Wandra Merrell, Roulette Records, 1960.
2. Daniel H. Pink, *The Power of Regret: How Looking Backward Moves Us Forward* (Riverhead Books, 2022).

Chapter 11: Tweaks to Maintain Momentum

1. Admiral William H. McRaven, *Make Your Bed: Little Things That Can Change Your Life . . . and Maybe the World* (Grand Central Publishing, 2017), 69.
2. Alli Worthington, in a coaching session with the author.
3. Voltaire, *La Bégueule: Conte Morale*, (Franç, Grasset, 1772), line 2.

ABOUT THE AUTHOR

Erin Port is a writer, entrepreneur, and mom of four who launched her brand, Simple Purposeful Living, in 2018 with the mission to equip busy and overwhelmed women with practical solutions for simplifying the cumbersome aspects of life management. When women simplify those areas, they create space for what truly matters.

Erin draws from her master's-level training as an educator to host a successful weekly podcast, *Simple Purposeful Living*. Erin has appeared on Magnolia Network's *Family Dinner*, Hallmark's Real Connections commercials, *The Crystal Paine Show*, *The Product Boss* podcast, and the *Paring Down* podcast, and her work has been featured on *The Pioneer Woman* and Money Saving Mom.

Erin has launched a line of products, including meal planners, cookbooks, and notebooks. She and her family live in Polk City, Iowa.

For more information about Erin and Simple Purposeful Living, please visit
simplepurposefulliving.com